Observation

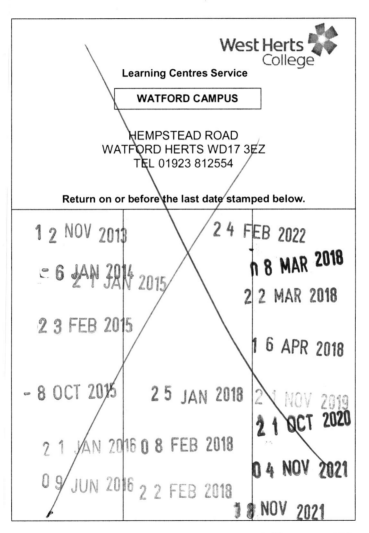

West Herts College

Learning Centres Service

WATFORD CAMPUS

HEMPSTEAD ROAD
WATFORD HERTS WD17 3EZ
TEL 01923 812554

Return on or before the last date stamped below.

Observation

Origins and Approaches
in Early Childhood

Valerie N. Podmore and Paulette Luff

Mc Graw Hill Open University Press

Open University Press
McGraw-Hill Education
McGraw-Hill House
Shoppenhangers Road
Maidenhead
Berkshire
England
SL6 2QL

email: enquiries@openup.co.uk
world wide web: www.openup.co.uk

and Two Penn Plaza, New York, NY 10121-2289, USA

First published 2012

A catalogue record of this book is available from the British Library

ISBN-13: 9780335244249 (pb)
ISBN-10: 0335244246 (pb)

Library of Congress Cataloging-in-Publication Data
CIP data has been applied for

Typeset by Aptara Inc., India
Printed in the UK by Bell and Bain Ltd, Glasgow.

Fictitious names of companies, products, people, characters and/or data that may be
used herein (in case studies or in examples) are not intended to represent any real
individual, company, product or event.

MIX
Paper from
responsible sources
FSC
www.fsc.org   FSC® C007785

The McGraw·Hill Companies

Contents

PART III
Observation as research

Acknowledgements

Val Podmore, 2006

A number of people had an invaluable influence on this book. I would like to express warm appreciation to all those colleagues who have contributed to observations in research and practice over the past decades. The substantive contributions of Anne Meade and Anne Smith warrant special mention here. Comments from students and teacher-researchers have continued to be helpful.

Some special contributions need chapter-by-chapter recognition. First, I would like to acknowledge Marie Bell, who was inspirational for Chapter 1. I am also very grateful to Helen May, who scrutinized the draft of Chapter 1 and made helpful suggestions. The innovative PhD work of Barbara Jordan, Sophie Alcock and Margaret Brennan warranted special mention in Chapter 2. And I warmly acknowledge Marilyn Fleer's work on sociocultural theoretical approaches and observations. Wendy Lee helpfully checked and provided the e-form for documenting a Learning Story (given in Table 6). Sue Cherrington and other colleagues of the School of Early Childhood Teacher Education, Victoria University, agreed to the use of unpublished material on running records for Chapter 3. Helpful feedback from Joy Cullen, Helen Hedges and Jane Bone contributed to Chapter 5, and I appreciated their enthusiastic approval to adapt and tabulate 'for observation purposes' their useful framework for ethics in research. Perspectives and reflections from Lesley Rameka and Sarah Te One contributed invaluably to the conclusion. Margaret Carr commented substantively on material about Learning Stories across a number of the chapters and provided important points of clarification and updating. Margaret also encouraged me to extend the section on Teaching Stories – I value her helpful suggestions and support.

Completing the original edition of this book was possible because I was able to spend several months of my research and study leave from Victoria University of Wellington researching, reflecting and writing, both overseas and back in Aotearoa. I warmly acknowledge Kay Morris Matthews, Head of the School of Education Studies, and the Leave Committee of the Faculty of Humanities and Social Sciences, Victoria University of Wellington.

Professors Chris Pascal and Tony Bertram were thoughtful hosts at the Centre for Research in Early Childhood (CREC) in Birmingham, England, where Mike

Gasper and Martin Hawthorne guided my journeys. Martin enthusiastically led me to the Baby EEL (the EEL and the BEEL are both discussed in Chapter 3).

Members and families of two early childhood centres of innovation (COIs) I work alongside have been encouraging and supportive (and are enthusiastic, reflective observers!).

Special thanks are due to David Podmore, Michelle and Kirsten, who were cheerfully supportive. David and Michelle both commented helpfully on draft chapters – during the summer holidays – and David provided good cooking and encouragement throughout the project and the journeys.

Paulette Luff, 2011

I am grateful to Val Podmore for having written such an engaging and informative book. My thanks to Open University Press for drawing my attention to the original text (published by NZCER Press) and for providing me with the opportunity to bring it to a new audience. I hope that the adaptation does justice to the first edition and facilitates its use in a wider context. Thank you to the three experienced reviewers who all made highly constructive suggestions for developing the new edition. Particular thanks to Senior Commissioning Editor Fiona Richman and Editorial Assistants Stephanie Frosch and Laura Givans who have supported and encouraged the project. I would also like to express gratitude to all those early years educators, students and colleagues who have contributed to my understanding of early childhood observation.

List of Tables

Introductions

Introduction to the new edition

Throughout the past century child observation has provided a focus for fruitful dialogues between early childhood educators from the United Kingdom and New Zealand/Aotearoa. As is shown in the first section of this book, common antecedents for child observation in both countries can be found in the philosophies of pioneer educators and the influence of early developmental psychology. The inspiration that was taken from Susan Isaacs' approach to pedagogy by New Zealand teachers in previous decades (discussed in Chapter 1) is paralleled today in UK educators' interest in, and admiration of, *Te Whāriki*, the curriculum for children aged from birth to school entry (Ministry of Education 1996) and the associated Learning Stories approach to assessment in early childhood settings (Carr 2001).

For those not familiar with *Te Whāriki* curriculum, the name translates from the Māori language as 'a woven mat for all to stand on' (May 2009: 245). The name also serves as a metaphor for the weaving of a bicultural curriculum, an encompassing of 'the diverse peoples, philosophies and services that participate in early education' (Anning *et al.* 2009: 21), and the intertwining of principles, strands and goals. The four principles are: empowerment; holistic development; family and community; and relationships. The five strands, with associated goals, are: belonging; well-being; exploration; communication; and contribution. The curriculum is based upon aspirations for children

> to grow up as competent and confident learners and communicators, healthy in mind, body, and spirit, secure in their sense of belonging and in the knowledge that they make a valued contribution to society.
> (Ministry of Education 1996: 9)

The aims and principles are expressed in both Māori and English and the curriculum document is published in both languages but there is no direct translation. It is ground-breaking as the first example of a national curriculum 'whose conceptual framework was based upon the cultural and political beliefs of the minority indigenous people' (Te One 2003: 36).

Observational assessments linked to *Te Whāriki*, the curriculum, take the form of Learning Stories (Carr 2001) that serve to document children's learning experiences (discussed in detail in Chapter 4). This form of assessment has led practitioners away from a deficit model of assessment towards a credit-based approach. The head teacher of a kindergarten reflected on the change: 'If a child couldn't hop you taught it. Now with *Te Whāriki* we were focusing on what they could do – working from where children were at' (Simpson cited in Te One 2003: 38).

Margaret Carr's (2001) book about Learning Stories is based upon a process of assessment originally defined by English academic Mary Jane Drummond (1993: 13) as 'the ways in which, in our every day practice, we observe children's learning, strive to understand it, and then put our understanding to good use'. In turn, Learning Stories have inspired the 'Learning Journey' approach to recording assessments, in England, where observation and response to child-initiated activities is an important element of the Early Years Foundation Stage curriculum framework (Department for Education and Skills 2007).

It is as a contribution to such professional dialogues that this book brings ideas and information about the history, theory and practice of child observation in New Zealand to new readers. It is hoped that through considering approaches from New Zealand, in parallel with insights from the practice of child observation within early childhood education in the UK, inspiration for respectful and appreciative approaches to observation, assessment and planning will be found.

Introduction to the first edition

In 1985, there was an article in New Zealand's *Playcentre Journal* about an observational study that took four years to complete. A key approach used in the research – a PhD study – was to observe 3-year-old children interacting with adults in early childhood centres in the greater Wellington region of New Zealand. In that study, observational categories were used, and the recorded and coded observations were then linked to aspects of the children's development. After the four-year study was completed, the short piece published about it in *Playcentre Journal* concluded with this statement from the researcher: ' "I still find observing children can be *fun*," said Val Podmore at the end of her study' (Warren 1985: 6).

This is still my view of observations. When I agreed to write this book I had in mind, first, that observing children can be fascinating and fun; second, that observations are important in understanding aspects of children's worlds; and third, that systematic observation is valuable as a key tool for assessing learning and teaching interactions.

This book explores the historical origins of observations and observational research, carried out for and by early childhood teachers in New Zealand. The book includes insights on how observations gained a place in early childhood education settings, traces the theoretical underpinnings of observational approaches, and presents newer research knowledge linked to sociocultural theories. It also illustrates a number of useful observational approaches, drawing on excerpts and examples from a range of recent New Zealand observational studies. The book refers to, and builds upon, existing groundwork: earlier international publications on observation and research methods; the short summary information on observation found in NZCER Press publications on research methods (Cardno 2003; Mutch 2005); and McMillan and Meade's (1985) classic introduction, *Observation: The Basic Techniques*.

The structure of the book

The contents of this book are organized into three sections, comprising six chapters and a conclusion. Part I looks at the historical and theoretical background. Chapter 1 sets out the context, describing historical trends and giving excerpts from conversations and interviews with Dr Marie Bell about her personal experiences of learning to observe in the United Kingdom during the late 1940s. It includes her vibrant account of how observing children came to be integrated into teacher education programmes in the United Kingdom and New Zealand. Chapter 2 focuses on the theoretical underpinnings of observation, culminating in a discussion of sociocultural approaches (including examples of studies).

Part II addresses the ways in which theory of observation translates into observational practice. Chapter 3 describes the qualitative and quantitative techniques of the observation process, drawing on a range of research studies to illustrate different approaches: from time sampling and category observations to running records, ethnography and narratives. Chapter 4 focuses specifically upon Learning Stories and Teaching Stories, explaining how these strategies work in a New Zealand context and their implications for practice in England and elsewhere.

Part III covers observation from the point of view of research. Chapter 5 focuses on ethics. It aims to foster Flinders's (1992) notion of 'ethical literacy', by addressing some ethical issues. It also looks at another framework – developed by Joy Cullen, Helen Hedges and Jane Bone (2005, 2009) – that raises questions to consider about observations. Chapter 6 covers the recording, analysis and reporting of observations (with emphasis on their intentions, purpose and use) and provides examples of these techniques for both qualitative and quantitative approaches. The place of information and communication technology (ICT) is also discussed.

The conclusion summarizes and draws together the major themes of the book. It includes personal accounts of observation in the voices of two experienced observers and gives some clear links to teaching practice.

Chapters 2 to 6 include a range of examples and vignettes from studies in New Zealand and the United Kingdom. We acknowledge warmly the wisdom and research work of everyone who has contributed, and those who continue to contribute, to our knowledge of observation.

Part I

Historical and theoretical background

1 Setting the context

This chapter defines observation and traces historical trends. It includes excerpts from discussions with Dr Marie Bell about her personal experiences of learning to observe in the United Kingdom during the late 1940s. Marie Bell gives a vibrant account of how observing children then came to be integrated into teacher education programmes in New Zealand. There is an exploration of the context for observing children in early years settings in the United Kingdom.

Observation – what is it?

Observation can be defined as the systematic watching and noting of people or phenomena. Anne Smith (1998: 6), when writing about understanding children through observing them, describes observation like this: 'Observation is a deliberate, active process, carried out with care and forethought, of noting events as they occur'.

More recently, Australian early childhood specialists Marilyn Fleer and Carmel Richardson (2004: 6) comment further that 'To us, observations are viewed as data – evidence of learning. The tool for gathering data is primarily "observation taking" – where the product and process are embedded.' An important point here is that if observations are to generate useful data about children, adults and the environment, and if they are to become a basis for making professional judgements about learning, teaching and educational programmes, they need to be systematic and planned.

This is not necessarily a simple task: 'Watching children as they learn and understanding their learning moments is complex and difficult work and places the highest of demands upon their educators' (Nutbrown and Carter 2010: 120). This book aims to illuminate the process, offering insights from both New Zealand and the United Kingdom.

Observation – the beginnings

During the 1890s developmental psychologists in the United States formed organizations to foster and publicize their research, teaching and practice.

G. Stanley Hall, the inaugural president of the American Psychological Association, was a key founder of the Child Study Association of America. An important aim of this organization was to make the findings of scientific child development research accessible to teachers, parents and the general public. These endeavours to promote research-based knowledge of child development became known as the American child-study movement. The influence of this movement soon spread internationally, reaching both the United Kingdom and New Zealand.

From the 1920s and 1930s, educational institutions co-opted various aspects of the child-study movement – for example, the application of its ideas to observations. This led people within the movement during that time, including Dr Susan Isaacs (1885–1948), to influence a new trend towards studying children through the use of observations.

Susan Isaacs, the head of an experimental school for children aged $2\frac{1}{2}$ to 10 years in Cambridge, England (Malting House School, 1924–27), was also an innovative teacher educator. The programme at her experimental school was a researched-based one. The research method used was the systematic observation, carried out by Isaacs and her assistant teachers, of the children at the school. In 1933 Isaacs accepted the part-time position of head of the new Department of Child Development at the Institute of Education in London, a position she held until 1943 (May 1997). She had a major influence on many educators – some travelled to London to study with her and found her a memorable teacher. For a number of others, Susan Isaacs's visit to New Zealand, sponsored by the New Education Fellowship, had a strong impact. Marie Bell recalls that

> Susan Isaacs's visit to Wellington in 1937 gave an impetus to the local child-study movement: her visit was sponsored by the New Education Foundation. Teachers were given time off to hear her lectures. Susan Isaacs's teaching methods encouraged active observation and enquiry.
>
> (Personal communication, 3 November 2005)

Also influential at this time was Dr Arnold Gesell, who worked at Yale University and the Gesell Institute in the United States. Arnold Gesell and his colleagues established many of the developmental norms for physical development that are still in use today.

The child-study movement resulted in the establishment of many 'laboratory schools' attached to universities and colleges of education. These schools enabled students to spend time working with and studying real children as part of their course work. The child-study movement promoted a focus on individual children that has continued to influence the fields of educational and psychological research up to the present day.

Marie Bell's story

During the 1940s and 1950s, Marie (Metekingi) Bell, a New Zealand-qualified teacher, was actively involved in the child-study movement. In 1949 she travelled to London to further her studies of early childhood teaching, and it was there that she learnt about systematically observing children to understand more about their development and interactions with other children and adults. Marie Bell studied at London University under Dorothy Gardner who was training students to be teacher educators and had herself worked with Susan Isaacs.

For one year, Marie Bell carried out observations in English nursery schools. One of these was Chelsea Nursery School in London, which, she remembers, was located in a house reputed to have been owned by King Henry VIII. Marie Bell recalls that at London University and Chelsea Nursery School there was a major emphasis on children's stages of development, and that Jean Piaget's theory had influenced the work of both Susan Isaacs and Dorothy Gardner. As she notes, however, there were some important differences between Piaget's and Isaacs's views on the stages of children's reasoning. Much of Isaacs's approach was based on her teaching and observations in the Malting House School in Cambridge, and she was also influenced by Gesell's maturational theory. However, Susan Isaacs, Dorothy Gardner and Marie Bell all criticized the fact that most of Gesell's work was confined to the laboratories of Yale University, and raised questions about the sampling methods involved in his research – the infants and children Gesell studied were almost all from the professional middle classes, and a number of the parents were members of the university staff. (These theoretical influences are discussed further in Chapter 2.)

In addition, Marie Bell remembers that Freud's psychoanalytic work was well known at London University, mainly through the influence of his daughter, Anna Freud. Psychoanalytic views of childhood had a major influence on Susan Isaacs, who was a follower of Melanie Klein. In her observational studies, for example, she focused strongly on children's emotional development and on the origins of their conflicts (Isaacs 1933).

The team at London University and Chelsea Nursery School was studying the friendships of children aged under 5 years. The observers used time sampling and carried notebooks in their pockets. Dr Marie Bell comments:

> We observed for 15 minutes at a time, focusing on kids who were friends. I got really sold on it!
> These observations were always followed by group discussion, led by people who knew the children better than we did. Their insights were valuable.
>
> (Personal communication, 20 February 2001)

The team's findings on friendship were that the 4-year-old children observed in the nursery school were not egocentric. They did have friends.

Marie Bell returned to New Zealand, bringing back with her both the new methods of observation and the idea of integrating observational techniques into teacher training programmes. In 1953 she was appointed a lecturer in junior education (of children aged 5–8 years) at the Wellington Training College. She recalls:

> The course for primary teachers lasted two years ... The course the senior woman, Irene Ely, and I planned and carried out was mainly focused on child development. Students were required to study a baby aged under 6 months of age at regular intervals. The study was monitored and discussed regularly. Those doing 'junior education' continued the study throughout their second year. Child study assignments were also set for students 'on section' [teaching practice], with a focus on the learning that was occurring – intellectual, physical, and emotional.
>
> (Personal communication, 3 November 2005)

From the 1950s, systematic observations were beginning to be used throughout New Zealand, partly through the innovations of Marie Bell and other lecturers at teachers' colleges, and partly through the new ideas evident in the training programmes of the playcentre and kindergarten movements.

Observation in early childhood education in New Zealand

In an early experiment in Christchurch, Dr C. E. Beeby and his wife Beatrice opened an outdoor playgroup for 5-year-olds (May 1997). In order to cut education spending during the Depression – the year was 1932 – children had been excluded from starting school until they were 6 years of age. Like Marie Bell, Dr Beeby was influenced by Susan Isaacs's approach. Beeby taught his tertiary students at Canterbury University College how to carry out systematic observations of 5-year-olds as part of their course work. Drawing mainly on Piaget's ideas, he wanted to check whether the young children engaged in outdoor play showed evidence of being egocentric – Beeby had his doubts about this. His students recorded the children's conversations, which on the whole were not egocentric during free play:

> Our preliminary results in observing children in the playground seemed to confirm my view; the proportion of egocentric language when they were doing things they had invented for themselves, and with companions of their choosing, was roughly half Piaget's figure.
>
> (Beeby 1992: 82)

In this way the observations that Beeby's students made, of 5-year-old children spontaneously playing in an outdoor setting, led to some reappraisal of Piaget's concept of egocentrism.

Dr Beeby was involved in the early development of the 'Playcentre' early childhood organization: 'In 1941 the playcentre movement had its birth in our living room' (Beeby 1992: 149). Certainly his wife, Beatrice, together with her two friends Joan Wood and Inge Smithells, were key founding members of playcentres in the Wellington region. During the late 1930s, there were various precursors of the playcentre (for example, one in Feilding, through the work of Gwen Somerset). Another was in Christchurch, where an English-trained nursery school teacher named Doreen Dolton was influential in running a nursery school attached to a secondary school (McDonald 1974; May 1997). Soon after this, Elizabeth Stewart Hamilton, who in 1947 studied with Susan Isaacs, opened a preschool centre at Karitane in Dunedin, where she introduced equipment for spontaneous play (May 1997). All four of these diverse regional initiatives had close philosophical ties to the New Education Fellowship, the group that had sponsored Susan Isaacs's visit to New Zealand in 1937.

Partly as a result of these contacts and influences, playcentre was the first early childhood education organization to make regular use of 'child study' observations in its training courses (Densem and Chapman 2000: 34). Advocates and practitioners of child-study observations – Gwen Somerset, Lex Grey, and Betty Odell – became leaders in this field and wrote guides for study that became part of playcentre training. These study guides, and other playcentre publications, included instructions and advice on how to prepare to observe (Grey 1975; Penrose 1998). The focus of these publications was on stages of development, particularly physical development.

Like Marie Bell, several key people in the playcentre movement were able to support the use of observations in primary schools and teacher education. Lex Grey lectured at Auckland Teachers' College from 1952. Furthermore, play-centre supervisors in Auckland advocated that allowance for a developmental period of self-selected play should be included throughout primary school, with trained observers observing children right into the upper primary-school classes (May 2009).

The Kindergarten College in Wellington also incorporated child study in its lectures, and included observing a baby in its practicum assignments (Hughes 1989). As Marie Bell recalls, in the early 1950s Joyce Barns, who was a leading light in the kindergarten movement at the time, travelled to England and did the same course that Marie had completed just a few years earlier. On Joyce Barns's return to Wellington, she took over the leadership of the Kindergarten College.

By the 1950s and 1960s, observation had become embedded into the practices of early childhood centres and into early childhood teacher training programmes. This meant that, as part of their daily work with children, many teachers were observing and analysing children's physical, social, emotional and cognitive/learning behaviour.

Observation in early childhood education in the United Kingdom

Early years education in the UK has several similarities with New Zealand, with a mixture of statutory, voluntary and private agencies contributing to the provision. There is a proud tradition of nursery schooling in the UK. In 1816 industrial reformer Robert Owen opened the first nursery school at New Lanark Mills, Scotland, so that young children under the age of 6 could be cared for while their parents worked in the cotton mill. In a later philanthropic venture, socialist campaigners Margaret and Rachel McMillan founded an open-air nursery school in Deptford. Their aim was to improve the health of poor children and provide them with educational opportunities.

Margaret McMillan used observation as a means of understanding and promoting children's development. She emphasized child study as a key element of the training of child carers and educators. Her trainees visited children in their homes to observe their growth and development, thus venturing outside the sheltered environment of the nursery school to understand the broader social circumstances in which the children and their families lived. In turn, the nursery school was designed to be seen and observed by the surrounding community (McMillan 1919).

McMillan's nursery school provided the model for the Chelsea Open Air Nursery School (opened in 1928 by Natalie Davis). Susan Isaacs became closely involved with this nursery school and it established strong links with her Department of Child Development, at London University. This was the Chelsea Nursery School that Marie Bell visited to observe in 1949 (see above).

Demand for nursery school places outstripped supply and, from the early 1960s, some mothers found a solution to this problem by setting up playgroups where their children could socialize with others and enjoy a variety of play experiences. Like Playcentre in New Zealand (see above), the Pre-School Playgroup Association (PPA) supported the setting up of community playgroups, run by parent committees, and they also organized training. Training courses allowed for the sharing of good practice and often involved observational child study work. In a video interview, to celebrate 50 years of the Pre-school Learning Alliance (formerly the PPA), founder Belle Tutaev spoke of the importance of 'standing up for children' and her aim

> . . .to give children the benefits of socializing and learning in a happy way. Not with checklists, because I'm dead against that sort of thing, because it's not 'one size fits all' with children . . . If you would just

think about it, what group of personalities would all fit together and be ticked on a ticklist? I do think that you should keep records of children's progress and interests and develop those interests into progress, that's what we used to do . . .

(Pre-school Learning Alliance 2011)

The importance of parent involvement in early childhood education was highlighted in the Rumbold Report (DES 1990). This influential report considered the diversity of provision in state nursery schools, playgroups, private nursery schools and private and local authority day nurseries, as well as with childminders. Two of the elements identified within the Rumbold Report as crucial for the provision of high-quality education for children under five were:

- collaborative planning which is based upon systematic and regular observation-based assessment of children in all areas of development;
- record keeping which is built upon contributions from educator, parent and child, and which feeds and supports children's learning.

(DES 1990: 35)

The use of observations to note and record children's progress, extend opportunities for learning, and provide stimulating learning environments is now formally incorporated within curriculum frameworks.

The place of observation in early years curricula

England

The first national curriculum for the early years in the UK was published in the same year as *Te Whāriki*. The *Desirable Outcomes for Children's Learning on Entering Compulsory Education* (SCAA 1996) set out goals to be achieved within six areas of learning, in preparation for school. These were soon reviewed and replaced by the *Curriculum Guidance for the Foundation Stage* (CGFS) (QCA 2000). The six areas of learning, and associated learning goals, remained but it included a new emphasis upon playful learning and an extension of an active, child-centred approach into the first year of school. *Birth to Three Matters* (DfES 2002) was subsequently introduced, as a framework to promote and support effective practice for those caring for babies and very young children. This included the advice to 'look, listen and note' children's positive responses (DfES 2002; Elfer 2005). These two framework documents, together with national standards for the registration and inspection of childcare, were combined within the Early Years Foundation Stage curriculum (EYFS) (DfES 2007).

Practitioners' observation skills were considered to be important for the successful implementation of the CGFS and this remains the case with the EYFS. Educators are required to:

- make systematic observations and assessments of each child's achievements, interests and learning styles;
- use these observations and assessments to identify learning priorities and plan relevant and motivating learning experiences for each child;
- match their observations to the expectations of the early learning goals.

(DfES 2007)

An Early Years Foundation Stage Profile is completed for each child to assess their attainment at the end of this phase of their education. It is based primarily upon judgements of observed behaviour during independent, child-initiated activities. Data for every child and school is collected by each local authority for the collation of national statistics. This forms baseline data to predict and judge the progress of each cohort of children and thus to measure the effectiveness of schools in adding value by boosting predicted attainment scores.

Within the EYFS, early years practitioners are required to use child observation in two different and potentially contradictory ways (Fawcett 2009; Luff 2012). On the one hand, they must use observations of children as a basis for planning open-ended learning opportunities in response to children's interests and, on the other hand, are required to record observations to chart each child's achievement according to preset learning outcomes. Early childhood curricula in the other countries of the UK also emphasize the use of observation for formative assessment but there is not the same requirement for a final summative assessment.

National early childhood curricula have developed in parallel in the four countries of the United Kingdom. Following political devolution in the late 1990s, governments in Northern Ireland, Scotland and Wales have all focused upon educational policy, and associated social reforms, as a means to enhance childhoods and increase opportunities for their citizens. In her book about the Early Years Foundation Stage, Ioanna Palaiologou (2010) provides a detailed summary of early years policy and provision in each of the countries of the British Isles. Information can also be found on each of the government websites. In every country the place of observation is recognized in the curriculum guidance.

Northern Ireland

In Northern Ireland, curriculum guidance for government-funded early years settings was first published in 1997. This has been updated to coincide with the introduction of a new practical and play-based Foundation Stage curriculum for 4- to 6-year-olds in primary schools. The *Revised Guidance for Pre-School Education* (DENI 2006) recommends that planning should be informed by ongoing observation of children. Observation forms the basis for assessment of children and reflection upon practice:

> In order to plan, prepare and organise good quality pre-school education, staff need to observe children at play, review and evaluate the curriculum regularly and maintain appropriate records. The information gained from these processes will enable staff to take account of the needs of individual children, offer suitable challenges and provide for progression in play activities.
>
> (DENI 2006: 7)

Scotland

In Scotland, a *Curriculum for Excellence* (Scottish Executive 2005) has been created to guide provision for all children aged 3–18 years. Seven key principles underpin curriculum design:

- challenge and enjoyment;
- breadth;
- progression;
- depth;
- personalization and choice;
- coherence;
- relevance.

(LTS 2011)

All of these require educators working with children in the 'Early Level' to be observant, in order to provide relevant active learning experiences and engage in meaningful dialogues with parents about children's progress. For the youngest children there is *Pre-Birth to Three* guidance (LTS 2010). This sets out four key principles: rights of the child; relationships; responsive care; and respect. One of the ways in which these are put into practice is through a careful cycle of observation, planning and assessment.

Wales

An innovation in early childhood education has been seen in Wales where a play-based *Foundation Phase* curriculum (WAG, 2008) has been introduced to provide for children from the ages of 3 to 7 years. Piloted and phased in gradually, it is now in place for the full age range with the intention of offering all children experiential learning activities in both indoor and outdoor environments. Once again, observation has a key place in curriculum planning and assessment:

> By observing children carefully to note their progress, involvement and enjoyment, as well as focusing on the attainment of predetermined outcomes, practitioners should be able to plan a more appropriate curriculum that supports children's development according to individual needs.
>
> (DCELLS 2008: 6)

The booklet *Observing Children* offers advice and practical examples of the use of observation in the Foundation Phase (DCELLS 2008). Observation is also a focus for practitioner training.

Summary

This chapter has identified the place of child observation in early childhood education in New Zealand and the United Kingdom and established elements of a shared history. This is further explored when considering common theoretical underpinnings, in the next chapter. The importance of observation within UK curriculum frameworks demonstrates a need for the sharing of good practice. A search for important insights from the holistic, empowering and inclusive approaches to observing children in *Te Whāriki* forms part of this quest for quality.

2 Understanding children through observations – where do the theories lead us?

The focus of this chapter is on the theoretical underpinnings of observing. It considers the contributions of Gesell's research and theoretical work on maturation, Piaget's constructivism, psychodynamic insights, behavioural approaches, Bronfenbrenner's ecological perspectives, and Vygotsky's cultural–historical/sociocultural views. The theoretical appraisals culminate in more recent sociocultural approaches, with examples drawn from research in New Zealand and the United Kingdom.

The child-study movement

Charles Darwin (1877) published an article based on observations of his son's first three years (recorded more than thirty years earlier). In this paper he provided detailed examples and analysis of various aspects of the child's physical, social and emotional growth. His theorizing provoked questions about the inherited nature of human capacities, as the following extract illustrates:

> When eleven months old, if a wrong plaything was given him, he would push it away and beat it; I presume that the beating was an instinctive sign of anger, like the snapping of the jaws by a young crocodile just out of the egg, and not that he imagined he could hurt the plaything. When two years and three months old, he became a great adept at throwing books and sticks, etc. at anyone who offended him; and so it was with some of my other sons.
>
> (Darwin 1877: 288)

Darwin's ideas were influential in the early years of the child-study movement and his involvement brought respect for the emerging science of developmental psychology (Fawcett 2009). In the 1890s, G. Stanley Hall (founder of the Child Study Association in the United States and first president of the

American Psychological Association) aimed to develop a theory of individual development that connected closely with Darwin's work on the evolution of the species (Lightfoot *et al.* 2009).

Arnold Gesell (who was a student of Stanley Hall) and Jean Piaget carried out in-depth studies of young children, using observations. Both Gesell and Piaget were familiar with the biological sciences, and they drew on this knowledge to develop detailed approaches to observing infants and children. As suggested in Chapter 1, Piaget's and Gesell's theories strongly influenced those people working in education who had begun to practise the systematic observation of children's behaviour.

Arnold Gesell

Arnold Gesell (1880–1961), a prominent American child psychologist and re-searcher who was also qualified as a doctor of medicine, explained the process of children's development as maturation of their innate capacities over time. He led a series of major observational studies of infants and children, and doc-umented infants' development repeatedly during their first years of life. From these descriptions he proceeded to prescribe specific developmental norms. His work was minutely detailed (for example, he described 53 'stages' of infants' rattle behaviour, which was just one of 40 different behaviours whose stages he wrote about in detail). According to Thelen and Adolph (1992), Gesell's ideas encompassed both genetic rigidity, as a maturationist, and – in contrast – the notion of individually different, active children. His theoretical concepts of maturation and the gradual unfolding of patterns of behavioural develop-ment, in which all children follow similar stages, may have paved the way for acceptance of Piaget's theory (Vasta *et al.* 1999) within the United States and beyond.

Gesell's major contribution to observational methods was to use photo-graphic recording and cinematography to generate catalogues and archives of visual data on infants' and children's behaviour. His rather rigid developmen-tal norms, derived from observations of largely middle-class and professional Anglo-American babies, influenced child development texts such as those pro-duced in the UK by Mary Sheridan (1973; Sheridan *et al.* 2008). Gesell's use of advanced photographic methods to observe infants and young children – see, for example, 'A pictorial survey of preschool behaviour' (Gesell 1950: 58–61) – makes him one of the forerunners of the innovative observational approaches evident in educational settings today, which use information and communi-cation technologies such as digital photography and video recording (see, for example, Collins *et al.* 2010; Webster 2010).

Jean Piaget

Swiss biologist and psychologist Jean Piaget (1896–1980) also observed children. Unlike Gesell's studies in the laboratories of Yale University and the Gesell Institute, many of Piaget's observations were of children in their everyday surroundings. He made detailed observational records of children (including his own), focusing mainly on growth and the development of thinking. He believed that infants and children construct their own knowledge and meanings through their activities and explorations of their environment. According to Piaget, an individual constructs new knowledge using three closely connected processes: *assimilation*, *accommodation*, and *adaptation*.

Assimilation is described as 'the use of existing structures to understand or interpret new experiences' (Smith 1998: 217), by absorbing new experiences into the individual's existing *schemas* (mental structures or models for action). Through accommodation – described as 'the adjustment of the organism to environmental demands through modification of existing structures' (Smith 1998: 217) – individuals modify their existing understanding (that is, their existing schemas) in order to integrate new experiences. Adaptation is the combined process of assimilation and accommodation, giving *cognitive equilibrium* or balance, and allowing the individual to reach new understandings (Piaget and Inhelder 1969).

Piaget (1968) wrote extensively about infants' and children's stages of intellectual development, which in brief summary include:

- the *sensorimotor* stage (birth to 2 years): divided into 6 substages, in which initially reflexes dominate and infants' knowing is linked to their senses and bodily movement;
- the *pre-operational* stage (2–6 years): this is marked by major language development evidencing the beginning of symbolic thought, but is a time when the child's thinking relies on perceptions;
- the *concrete operations* stage (6–12 years): the child groups objects logically, comes to understand the concept of conservation (of number, liquid, mass, etc.) and can appreciate others' points of view; and
- the *formal thought* stage (from around the age of 12 years): this is characterized by hypothetical thinking and abstract verbal reasoning.

Piaget's understandings of young children's learning have been widely applied in educational contexts. In England, the Plowden Report (HMSO 1967) advocated a child-centred approach to education; in the United States the High Scope approach (Weikart *et al.* 1971), similarly, emphasizes active learning experiences; and Piaget's influence can also be seen in the programmes and observational focus of New Zealand early childhood services during the 1940s to 1970s

(Hill *et al.* 1998; Smith 1998). Cunningham (2006), drawing upon oral history testimony of English early years teachers who trained prior to 1955, identifies the 'towering figure of Piaget' in informing curriculum and contributing to a 'distinctive shift in teacher–child relationships' (p. 15).

Piaget's theories provided a basis for the Froebel Research project, led and reported by Chris Athey (1991). Five thousand detailed observations of 2- to 5-year-old children, who attended an especially designed enrichment project, were collected over a two-year period. Athey worked with her colleagues, and with the children's parents, to identify their persistent interests revealed in systematic patterns of behaviour, or 'schemas', during their play. These observations were used as a basis for mapping the schematic development of individual children and identifying age-related behaviour patterns within the group. The children who participated in the project showed significant gains in performance on standardized intelligence tests.

Athey's work has provided a basis for interpreting young children's thoughts and actions and making sense of observed behaviours (e.g. Nutbrown 2006). In some early years settings the identification of schemas, through careful observations of children's play by educators and families, forms a basis for curriculum planning. This is exemplified in work at the Pen Green Centre (Mairs 1990; Whalley *et al.* 2007). Cath Arnold (1999, 2003) provides extended examples of interpreting observations in this way, in her accounts of her grandchildren's early learning.

Insights from psychodynamic theory

In contrast to Gesell and Piaget, Freud ([1940] 2001) gave an account of human development that was not based on observations of children but upon his interpretations of his adult clients' descriptions of incidents during childhood. Freud's ideas, about the impact of the unconscious mind on behaviour and the significance of early experiences for the development of personality, have had influence upon early childhood education in England. This is partly through the work of Susan Isaacs (see Chapter 1). As a trained psychoanalyst, she completed detailed observations of the children at her Malting House experimental school in order to understand their social and emotional growth (Isaacs 1933).

Esther Bick (1964) later pioneered methods of infant observation underpinned by psychodynamic theory. This form of observation is referred to as the Tavistock Method (named after the clinic where it was developed). It usually involves weekly, one-hour long visits to a family home in order to follow the development of a baby or very young child throughout a year of her or his life (Miller *et al.* 1989; Briggs 2002). The approach to observation is challenging, as the observer aims to be neutral and non-participant yet fully tuned in to the infant's inner thoughts and feelings and the emotions that the observation provokes. No notes are taken but very close attention is paid to the non-verbal signals of the infant and the features of any interaction between the child and parents, particularly the mother. A detailed account of the session is written up in which, as far as possible, the complete sequence of events is recalled and described. Widely used in psychotherapy training, and for the continuing professional development of social workers (Trowell and Miles 1991), more recently this form of observation has been used in work with early years educators (Elfer 2005, 2007; Elfer and Dearnley 2007).

Peter Elfer (2005, 2007) suggests that understandings from psychodynamic theory could also inform methods of child observation in child care settings. He expresses concern that observation records often focus upon cognitive development and that the strong feelings of young children and their carers are neglected. In his research, professionals who observed babies and toddlers using an adapted form of the Tavistock Method found it to be a powerful means of relating to the children and getting close to their experiences.

Behavioural approaches

Behavioural approaches, by contrast, were developed in the United States as a more rigorously scientific approach than psychodynamic theory. With a strict focus on observed behaviours, in the 1950s behaviourist theorists conducted observation in controlled experimental conditions that required laboratory settings and structured situations or preselected play equipment.

While followers of B. F. Skinner focused on observing and reinforcing children's social behaviour, another social learning theorist, Albert Bandura, and his colleagues developed observational learning theory. Bandura (1977) theorized that children learn through observing and imitating others. He carried out a series of laboratory-based studies in which he observed young children imitating aggressive behaviour or (in some experiments) more altruistic behaviour, in response to viewing an adult's behaviour (such as hitting a rubber Bobo doll, or placing a coin in a box marked as designated for a benevolent society). Bandura's early work involved observing children in structured situations; later, he moved to observing in more natural situations and settings. He also developed the theoretical concept of self-efficacy, or people's belief in their own capabilities (Bandura 1997).

By the 1970s and 1980s, researchers and teachers quite frequently questioned the ecological validity of laboratory studies. Teachers and parents wanted to know more about what happens in real-life situations. Many studies, including those with behavioural underpinnings, had moved to natural settings such as homes, schools and early childhood centres. Behavioural theory foreshadowed the proliferation of many classroom observational studies, in which researchers observed, recorded and analysed children's and teachers' behaviour. A notable early contribution of behaviourism was the notion of objectivity and 'unbiased' observations. Behaviourists believe objectivity is desirable in order to minimize observer bias. In order to be objective, observers remain neutral and distance themselves from the people and activities under observation. The following reflections explore further views on objective observations.

Objectivity

By undertaking systematic observations of children, observers move beyond reliance on impressions that can be coloured by their own specific values and beliefs. When we carry out careful observations, we develop skills in using objective rather than subjective language and are able to separate out children's actual actions from what we think or feel about what they are doing (see Papatheodorou *et al.* 2011). Being more objective means suspending judgements until detailed observations have been gathered on several separate occasions.

As Anne Smith (1998: 41) explains, being 'objective' also implies 'the need to be conscious of self and to be critically self-aware of the meanings we bring to the process of observation'. Interpretations of observations tend to reflect the observer's values and views of the world. We all carry our own preconceived ideas about people, and these can include the children with whom we work and the people we observe. There may be differences between our world views and those of the children we are observing and their families and communities.

Subjectivity

More recently, Anne Smith has also raised questions about the extent to which observers can be totally objective. After reflecting on feminist writings, Smith (1998: 41) concedes that 'there is no such thing as a pure, value-free, objective approach to observing human behaviour'. Marilyn Fleer believes that what we value influences what we observe: 'Our observations are always subjective and reflect those things that we value' (Fleer and Richardson 2009: 138). She notes, for example, that in a centre in which literacy is valued, teachers will document children's early literacy attempts. Peter Elfer (2005) goes further in suggesting that subjective responses are important for developing sensitivity, helping observers to develop a sense of connection with young children, to appreciate their points of view and understand and contain emotions.

Some suggestions for observational practice

- If we suspend judgements, we may be more able to concentrate on what is actually happening, and see children's strengths, interests and learning experiences more clearly and in context.
- Alongside our records of observations, it can be useful to include personal reflections on both the focus and the process. It is important to develop and show awareness of how our own feelings and understandings may influence our interpretations of what we observe.

Ecological and sociocultural perspectives

Urie Bronfenbrenner

Urie Bronfenbrenner (1917–2005) developed an ecological model of human development. He criticized the way child development research had focused on individual children's behaviour towards strangers in strange settings, which influenced the move towards observing in homes, schools and early childhood centres. Bronfenbrenner (1979, 1986, 2004) postulates that a person develops within a series of five systems in the environment. These systems are, in increasing order of size or complexity:

- the *microsystem* – the immediate environment of the family and community;
- the *mesosystem* of social institutions – for example, education settings, early childhood centres, schools, classrooms;
- the *exosystem* – an external system that connects micro- and mesosystems and affects children indirectly (for example, parents' workplace);
- the *macrosystem* – including cultural, economic and political systems, together with global changes; and
- the *chronosystem* – the changes that take place over time in an individual's life and at different points in history.

Bronfenbrenner's theory has influenced approaches to observation in several key ways. One has been the move to study children and adults in natural environments and everyday settings. Another has been the emphasis within curriculum documents upon both the learner and the learning environment (Ministry of Education 1996; DfES 2007). A third has been the attention in policy to children's families and the wider social environment in which children are growing up (Ministry of Education 2002; DfES 2004a, 2004b).

Lev Vygotsky

There are also sociocultural reasons for observing children. Sociocultural theories are linked to the work of the Russian educational psychologist Lev Vygotsky (1896–1934). Vygotsky's (1978) pioneering work on the cultural and historical contexts of learning contributes to understandings of how children see the world and their own experiences. He conceived children's learning as being a social process, guided, modelled and structured by adults and more experienced peers.

Vygotsky's theory connects learning to the history and culture of groups, including minority groups (Cullen 2001). Vygotsky (1978) emphasized that the contexts of social interaction and children's learning were influenced by understanding the culture(s) that surround them. From a sociocultural perspective, understanding their culture(s) is an integral part of young children's learning. In turn, teachers' understanding of children's cultural and language experiences is part of fostering an effective learning relationship. Sociocultural observations characteristically emphasize researching and understanding children within their sociocultural contexts, which are dynamic, are embedded in historical traditions, and evolve and change over time (Rogoff 2003; Fleer *et al.* 2009).

Vygotsky proposed that children learn most effectively within the 'zone of proximal development'. This zone lies slightly beyond the level of the child's independent competence, so that learning takes place when the child is guided by more competent others (Vygotsky 1978). This zone is the area of learning and development, or the difference between what a child can do alone and with assistance.

Barbara Rogoff

From Vygotsky's perspective, understanding culture is integral to children's learning, and other sociocultural perspectives emphasize that learning culture involves participating in it with others. Barbara Rogoff in the United States, for example, proposes that development is 'a process of transformation through people's participation rather than of acquisition' (Rogoff *et al.* 1995: 46). Other recent research, including work by Barbara Rogoff, introduces the concepts of shared understanding, joint problem solving and active co-construction of learning (Rogoff 1990, 1998; Siraj-Blatchford *et al.* 2002; Jordan 2009; Podmore 2009).

Arapera Royal Tangaere

In Aotearoa New Zealand, Arapera Royal Tangaere's (1996: 111) research high-lights how 'Māori human development is embodied in *te ira tangata* ("the prin-ciple of people")'. She has applied both Bronfenbrenner's ideas about ecological systems and Vygotsky's concept of the zone of proximal development to under-standing children's learning and development in a *kōhanga reo* (Māori kinder-garten) context. In the discussion of her findings from a considerably in-depth observational study of a child's experiences of *te kōhanga reo*, Royal Tangaere (1997) explains that being part of the *kōhanga reo* environment enables a child to absorb Māori language, culture and social roles through participation in rou-tines from *mihimihi* (greetings), *karakia* (prayers), and *waiata* (songs), or *haka* (dance). As Royal Tangaere demonstrates, immersion in *te reo*, the Māori lan-guage, is essential for this process to take place.

A valuing of a cultural and historical heritage is also seen in *Curriculum Cymreig*. This part of the national curriculum in Wales reflects the history, geography, creative arts, language and literature of the country. In the Founda-tion Phase curriculum this is integrated across all areas of learning and through Welsh language programmes. In the evaluation of the implementation of the Foundation Phase curriculum, in which the ECERS-E rating scale was used (see Chapter 3), a specific Curriculum Cymreig subscale was designed. Perhaps un-surprisingly, Welsh-medium settings scored more highly than English-medium settings on this measure of cultural awareness (Siraj-Blatchford *et al.* 2006). There is increasing provision of Welsh-medium education in all sectors. In addition to state provision, a voluntary organization, *Mudiad Meithrin*, provides Welsh-medium playgroups (*Cylch Meithrin*) and day nurseries (*Meithrinfa Dyddiol*) and runs parent and toddler groups (*Cylch Ti a Fi*) where parents/carers and children can come to speak Welsh or to learn Welsh, if they are not native speakers.

Scaffolding and co-construction

Scaffolding and co-construction are two different but related theoretical con-cepts derived from Lev Vygotsky's work to describe types of teaching and learn-ing interactions. Jerome Bruner and his colleagues in the United States first used 'scaffolding' as a metaphor for a teaching and learning process, drawing on the idea of a supportive scaffold used by builders. Scaffolding describes a teaching and learning situation in which a more experienced person – a teacher, tutor, other adult, or peer – supports learning by working within the learner's zone of proximal development. The teacher 'scaffolds' the child towards the level at which the child is capable of working with assistance, beyond what the child can achieve without support (Wood *et al.* 1976). The concept of 'scaffolding' has been critiqued as a rigid model, placing the teacher in a position of power over the student (Rogoff 1998; Jordan 2009).

More equal sharing of power and joint contributions to learning are incorporated in the concept of 'co-construction'. Barbara Jordan, who observed teachers using scaffolding and co-construction with children in early childhood centres, found that teachers listened more, and more often planned collaboratively with children, when they made use of sociocultural theory and the notion of co-construction. As Jordan (2009: 51) comments:

> In contrast to scaffolding, the language of co-construction of learning generally has no prescribed content outcomes (the teacher has no specific direction of learning in mind); the focus is on developing shared meanings/intersubjectivity, and [on] each participant contributing to the ongoing learning experiences from their own expertise and points of view.

Active participation in meaning making and shared learning experiences for learners and teachers are also emphasized in 'sustained shared thinking' (Siraj Blatchford *et al.* 2002; Siraj-Blatchford 2010). This strategy involves educators and learners extending their thinking through open dialogue about a question or problem, with both parties contributing and developing ideas. It is a notable feature of practice in early years settings identified as excellent in quality and is associated with positive outcomes for children's learning. It requires educators to be observant so that they tune in to children's interests and quickly become aware of opportunities for this type of interaction.

Many other studies in New Zealand and the United Kingdom are underpinned by sociocultural theories. Sophie Alcock's (2005) observational research included an emphasis on the playfulness of children and adults in early childhood centres. These observations extend our views of what we observe in early childhood centres to include more imaginative and humorous aspects of children's communication. The sophistication and complexity of children's thinking, and the need for educators to pay close attention to ways in which meanings are signified in imaginative play, is also shown by Maulfry Worthington (2010). She draws particular attention to 'imagination as an act of dynamic change' in which children, as central players in games involving new media technologies, create and operate imaginary gadgets to effect change.

Other parts of children's lives in early childhood centres include studies of routines, and the shared culture of mealtimes and meal preparation in early childhood centres (e.g. Brennan 2005; Albon 2007), and observational research on children's rights and participation (e.g. Te One 2005; Kanyal and Cooper 2012).

The main theoretical influences on approaches to observation are summarized in Table 2.1.

Table 2.1 Theoretical influences on approaches to observation

Name	Theory	Key theoretical concepts	Influences on observation
Gesell	Maturation	Developmental norms 'Unfolding of patterns of development'	Child study; photographic recording
Piaget	Constructivist	Processes: assimilation, accommodation, adaptation, cognitive equilibrium Stages: sensorimotor, pre-operational, concrete operational, formal thought 'Development drives learning'	Child study; observing children's play (influenced training and practice across the early childhood sector and schools)
(Skinner) Bandura	Behavioural	Social learning; observational learning; modelling	Objectivity; interobserver reliability (influenced classroom behaviour studies)
Freud Bick	Psychodynamic	Unconscious mind affects behaviour Psychosexual stages of human development	Tavistock method of close observation
	Feminist	Reflexivity (reflecting on how the observer's personal history influences recent decisions or views)	Personal reflections; questioning of 'objectivity'
Bronfenbrenner	Ecological	Context: ecological validity Five systems: microsystem, mesosystem, exosystem, macrosystem, chronosystem	Ecological validity: observation of people in everyday activities in naturalistic settings; its influence on assessment and evaluation in relation to *Te Whāriki*
Vygotsky Bruner Rogoff	Cultural-historical / sociocultural	Culture, language, teaching and learning within the zone of proximal development 'Learning drives development' Co-construction of meaning	Cultural contexts Underpins assessment in relation to *Te Whāriki*

Summary

An overall aim of observations in educational settings is to contribute to providing high-quality education. Clearly, many theories and theorists have influenced ideas about observation, and ways of carrying them out. Systematic observation, and sociocultural approaches to observing in early childhood settings, can lead us to:

- understand children's strengths and interests, and what they are capable of understanding and doing. By systematically observing children with their peers, teachers and other adults, teachers, researchers and teacher-researchers can help to understand and respond to children's interests, their strengths, and where they may need further support to foster their learning and development;
- participate sensitively in children's learning, leading to co-construction of learning experiences;
- link theory with practice and appraise ideas. Our theoretical knowledge helps us to analyse and interpret what our observations might mean, and to plan our programmes;
- connect closely with early childhood curricula;
- assess children's learning – observation is the key tool that we use for gaining information for assessment;
- evaluate our teaching practice. The intention is to become reflective practitioners who are attuned to children and who understand young children's perspectives and their learning and development;
- understand aspects of children's worlds; and
- practise more inclusive strategies for diverse learners in classrooms and early childhood education settings.

Part II

From theory to practice

3 Processes – how to observe?

A first step to observation is choosing an appropriate approach. This chapter describes a range of practical observational techniques, both quantitative and qualitative. It draws on a variety of examples from research to illustrate different approaches. These range from time sampling, category observations and rating scales to running records, ethnography and narrative approaches.

Observation techniques

Different types of observational approaches are useful for different purposes. Whether an approach is appropriate depends on the nature of the research question to be answered, and/or the type of assessment or evaluation required. Observational techniques can be either quantitative or qualitative (or both).

Quantitative observations

Quantitative observations usually involve numerical data (numbers – including, for example, calculated incidents or numbers of specific behaviours, interactions or events). They also include ratings of behaviour and experiences in the environment. The observer may use precoded or preselected categories of behaviour or interactions. Reliability is important: for example, *interobserver reliability*, in which, ideally, two or more observers independently record very similar observational data when observing the same behaviour. Reporting the *stability* (consistency) of the observations is also important – for example, the extent to which observational records, usually made by the same observer, are consistent across different observational days.

Qualitative observations

Qualitative observations are usually recorded in words, by observers who may be non-participants, or participants in the observational setting. For example, a teacher observing in his or her own early childhood centre or classroom will be a participant observer, whereas a visitor (whether teacher or researcher) to a centre or classroom is likely to be a non-participant observer.

Validity

Validity is important. In particular, the observations should be validated by the participant(s) in a process described as 'respondent validation' (Foster 1996: 101). There is also increasing recognition of the role of young children in validating their own research data (Cullen *et al.* 2005).

More information about reliability, validity and robustness in observational studies is given in Chapter 6. The next sections of this chapter provide details, appraisals, and examples from research and practice of both the quantitative and qualitative approaches to observation.

Quantitative approaches

Two clear decisions are needed before commencing systematic quantifiable observations:

- What behaviours or types of interactions are to be observed?
- How will the observations be timed?

Choosing what to observe

The behaviours, events or characteristics to be rated are determined in advance and clearly defined, and are often precoded. Precoded observation means that, before starting to observe, the observer plans and selects specific categories of behaviour. It is then possible to record the occurrence of these precoded categories when actually observing on site, or when observing video excerpts.

Table 3.1 describes some precoded behavioural categories used when observing young children in classrooms.

Timing observations

The observations need to take place for long enough to collect meaningful and stable samples of behaviour or interactions. Time is also needed for the observer's presence and/or the observation process to become familiar and fairly unobtrusive. It is important for observations to be timed and organized in a way that answers the research question(s), and/or is appropriate to fit in with the observer's teaching and other responsibilities.

Event recording

This approach records the occurrences of behaviour of interest (or target behaviour) over a specified period of time. Event recording is a way of collecting

Table 3.1 Precoded behavioural categories for observation

Attending
The child is on task: for example, looking at the teacher conducting the lesson or at a peer responding to the teacher.

Interaction with peer, positive
The child is interacting with a peer about task-relevant material: for example, during a morning talk.

Volunteering
Either by handraising or verbally, the child volunteers information, in response to a question addressed to the class or to provide task-relevant information.

Enthusiastic physical involvement
The child is actively involved in response to the task: for example, by spontaneously clapping hands or running to look at the teacher's book.

Note: These are 4 of 18 behavioural categories that were used in an early study of children in new entrant classrooms (Podmore 1978: 25–6).

data about a specific behaviour when the time available for observation is limited, and there is a particular behaviour of concern or interest, such as biting, bullying or excluding (or including) other children. Before the observations are begun, the event to be observed must be clearly defined.

Often the event is recorded quantitatively – for instance, the number of times it occurs. An example of quantitative event recording is set out in Table 3.2. This example focuses on inclusion and exclusion events.

Table 3.2 Recording inclusion and exclusion events

Date and time: Monday 8 September, 9 am – 3 pm		
Child	**Includes other/s**	**Excludes other/s**
James	1	1
Sarah	1111	1
Jacob	11	
Ben		
Jade	1	
Jane	1	

As shown in the example, event recording is a relatively simple way of looking at the frequency of certain behaviours. It can be useful if a behaviour is of concern (e.g. excluding other children), or as a way of focusing on a particular strength shown by a child or adult (e.g. including other children). It can help to test whether perceptions of a child are accurate. The teacher may be under the impression that James (see Table 3.2) is a child who excludes others from his play but evidence from the observation reveals only one instance of this behaviour, balanced by a positive incident of including others.

One disadvantage is that, by focusing on just one type of event, all of the other behaviours and interactions that take place are lost from the observational record. Another disadvantage is that the event is likely to be recorded out of context unless there is a record of what happens before it (the antecedent, or precedent) and what goes on after it (the consequence).

As an alternative to counting the occurrences of events, a narrative observation recorded in writing may also focus on a specific event or events. Table 3.3 shows a narrative approach to event recording that includes antecedents and consequences (narrative approaches are explained later in this chapter). As in the previous example of event recording, the behaviours under scrutiny are those of children including and excluding others.

Table 3.3 Event recording (including antecedents and consequences)

Children's names: James (Sarah, Jacob, Ben, Jade and Jane)
Date and time: 8 November, 9 am

Antecedent event	Exclusion/inclusion behaviour	Consequent event
James, Sarah and Jacob are jointly involved in moving wooden blocks and planks together on the floor. Sarah says: 'This is our train track.' Ben runs up to the group and kicks the blocks and planks.	James says to Sarah and Jacob: 'Ben's not coming on our train.' (Exclusion)	Ben walks away sucking his thumb.
Jane and Jade arrive, look at the 'train track' and Jane says: 'That's the train to Preston!'	Jacob passes a block each to Jane and Jade. (Inclusion)	James, Sarah, Jacob, Jane and Jade are jointly involved in adding blocks and planks. They make the 'train track' longer.

Teachers may also use event recording to monitor their own behaviour. In one example, given by Caryl Hamer (1999: 41), an early childhood centre supervisor wanting to monitor her own 'negative or restrictive behaviour' carried counters in one pocket. Throughout the day, whenever she made a negative statement she transferred a counter to another pocket.

Writing notes in a notebook about an event under scrutiny takes more time, but is useful in event recording because the observer can write brief notes about the time, the people present, and the context of the event. By writing down more details the centre supervisor might find, for example, that she or he uses 'negative or restrictive behaviour' only during other staff members' lunch breaks, when the ratio of adults to children is lower than at other times of the day. Event recording, including 'self-monitoring' of behavioural interactions, is more useful for effecting future change if it includes some written notes about antecedents and any precipitating interactions or events.

Categories of behaviour and interactions: frequency recording

These observations are structured and planned in detail. Observers using this quantitative technique calculate the number of times precoded categories of behaviour occur within a certain amount of time. When using precoded categories, it is necessary to know in advance exactly which behaviours are to be the focus of the observations. This means that before the formal observations are started definite decisions are needed about which categories are to be included in the set. Category observations, using a set of multiple behaviours, can be rather complex. Each behaviour is recorded as it occurs. Each category should be carefully defined, with clear examples given, and checked with another observer for reliability.

Since the process of developing the categories is so complex, once a clearly defined set of categories has been developed for one study, the same set tends to be adapted and used for subsequent studies in different locations. Following Ned Flander's (1960) development of a practical tool to observe and code interaction in classrooms, category observations that analysed students' (and teachers') behaviour were used extensively in educational research (e.g. Sylva *et al.* 1986; see below). A significant UK example was the *ORACLE* (Observational Research and Classroom Learning Environment) study (Galton *et al.* 1980, 1999) that offered an analysis of teaching styles and pupil types.

A study of infants and toddlers in New Zealand childcare centres (Podmore and Craig 1991) reported observations of 36 individual children at six different childcare centres. In that study, we used both frequency recordings and ethnographic/narrative observations. A set of 16 precoded interaction categories was adapted from Carollee Howes's research in California (Howes 1986). The observational chart in Table 3.4 shows what the interaction categories were, and how the frequencies of the category observations were recorded. As shown on the chart (see Table 3.4), the number and gender of the staff members and the number of children present were also noted.

The categories of observation that occurred most often were: infants' solitary activities, caregiver talk, infant interacts with peers, and caregiver touches/hugs/holds (infant). There were no major differences in girls' and boys' interactions across the categories. The early childhood teachers touched, hugged or held the infants more than twice as often at some centres than at others, and this might have reflected the different philosophies of the centres. The excerpt in Table 3.5 describes and illustrates some of the categories observed most frequently in the study (Podmore and Craig 1993: 19–20).

The advantages of category observations are that complex sets of categories and behaviours can be observed and recorded, and that both the frequency and the duration of behaviours can be calculated (that is, both the number of times a behaviour occurs and the length of time it goes on). It is possible to include both the child's and the adult's behaviour and interactions, rather than focusing simply on one child. The disadvantages are that observations concentrate on the predetermined categories of interaction only, so that other information may be missed; time is needed for training observers and recording reliable observations; and observations tend to be dyadic – focused on pairs rather than on groups of people.

Duration recording

This type of observation records how long a certain behaviour lasts, or how long children or adults are engaged in a task. As Anne Smith (1998: 59) notes, duration recording 'is most useful for behaviour that is relatively continuous or occurs at a high rate', like time spent crying, or time spent in a sandpit. Duration recordings have been used, for example, when teachers are concerned that an infant or young child is unsettled during transition, or a child appears to be engaged at a computer for long periods of time.

Duration recordings may also be used to check the extent to which girls and boys have equal access to certain activities or equipment. They may also be used to record the duration of a teacher's presence in specific areas of an early childhood centre. In an early, influential study, in New Zealand, Anne Meade and Frances Staden (1985) used an action research intervention to increase 4-year-old girls' participation in mathematical activities. Participants came from five kindergartens, located in three different cities. At the beginning of their study, Meade and Staden observed the teachers and recorded the amount of time they spent in different areas of the kindergartens. As shown in Table 3.6,

Table 3.4 Observation sheet for caregiver–infant interactive behaviour

Centre No: 11 No. of caregivers present: 2 Observer V.P. Date: 12 May 1990
Infant No: 16 No. of infants/children present: 6 Time: 10.15 am

Caregiver behaviours
Facilitative social interaction responses

Infant/toddler behaviours

Talk	Play	Mediates objects	Touch/ hug/ hold	Express positive affect	Positive response to social bid	Ignores request, negative response	Talks/ Babbles to careg.	Touches/ hugs careg.	Shares object with careg.	Express positive affect to careg.	Express negative affect to careg.	Asks careg. for object	Violates adult standards	Interacts with peers	Solitary activity
1															
1															
				1						1					
					1										
														1	
			1					1						1	
			1						1					1	
											1				
1				1			1								
Totals															
3	0	0	2	2	1	0	1	1	1	1	1	0	0	3	0

Note: This 'infant's' record was prepared as an example only.
Source: Podmore and Craig (1991: 80, adapted from Howes 1983).

Table 3.5 Frequently observed interactions

Infants and toddlers in the childcare centres of Aotearoa/New Zealand

---

Caregiver talk

Caregiver talks to child (exclude talk which is restricting, forbidding or an initial response to a request).

Examples: 'What colour would you like?' 'Would you like yellow?' 'We'll put it up so you can take it home later.' '[Infant's name], look at the drums.'

Infant interacts with peers

Child interacts verbally or non-verbally with other children.

Examples: Toddler reaches for a toy in a peer's hand; toddler asks peer 'What's that?'; infant touches toddler; older child holds infant on lap; toddler models/imitates adult's activity with peer; infant and peer gaze reciprocally at each other.

Caregiver touches/hugs/holds

Caregiver spontaneously touches, hugs or holds infant/toddler.

Examples: Caregiver places an arm around toddler; caregiver hugs infant; caregiver holds toddler on lap; caregiver carries infant in arms; caregiver carries infant in backpack; caregiver strokes infant's arm/legs.

Table 3.6 Where the teachers spent most time (non-intervention stages)

Collage, cutting and pasting	124	Car cases, forts, ladders and reels	68
Dough	117	Water	45
Painting or finger painting	70	Sandpit	35
Books	68	Carpentry (sometimes on a verandah)	31
Blocks	68		
Puzzles	54		
Family corner	35		
Table toys – Lego, Sticklebricks, etc.	33		
Crafts	30		

Notes:

1. Blocks and car cases scores may have been boosted because the researcher was present in the five kindergartens.

2. The three highest scores are not mentioned here. They were for general supervision, putting out or clearing away equipment, or talking to adults/children without being involved in a curriculum area.

Source: Meade and Staden (1985: 10).

the researchers found that the teachers spent much of their time with the play dough and collage, which traditionally tended to be more 'female'-oriented activities at early childhood centres.

Meade and Staden (1985: 13) noted that their observations throughout the study included duration recordings:

> The observers observed for 10-minute spans in each area alternatively, noting the names of children and adults present each minute when a beeper-timer went off. Around ten observation schedules were completed each [morning kindergarten] session, weather permitting.

The next step in their research was to focus their observations and interventions on two selected 'curriculum areas' – the blocks and the car case areas in the kindergartens. The duration recordings enabled the observers and researchers to report on the amount of time the girls spent in the blocks and car case areas before, during and after an intervention. Meade and Staden calculated the average length of time each child spent in each of the two areas at each stage of the study. One of their main findings was that the average duration of girls' time in the block areas increased during the intervention period.

Interval recording

In interval recording, the total observation time is divided into equal time slots or intervals. Time is usually allocated both for observing and for recording. For example, the observation slot may be 10 seconds to look for an occurrence of the category or categories of behaviour (an example of the kinds of behaviours that can be used for categories is given under the heading 'Choosing what to observe' earlier in this chapter). This is followed by a 5-second interval to record the behaviour(s) by ticking the chart, then another 10-second observation interval, and so on.

We used this method to time the category observations in our study of infants and toddlers in childcare centres. We observed each infant for 40 minutes on each of two separate days. As longer intervals are needed for more complex sets of interaction categories, we observed each child's behaviour and interactions with staff members for 15 seconds, then spent 15 seconds ticking the appropriate category code and writing down other contextual details, then we observed again, and so on, for 40 minutes. (An example of this kind of recording of observations is shown in Tabe 3.4, above.) We used a beeping timer to mark the intervals in our observations of the infants and toddlers.

Table 3.7 Time sampling: observations of co-operative behaviour

Child: Hasina		Location: Childcare Centre	
Date: 15 November, morning		Weather: Fine, sunny	

Time	Behaviour	Interacting with	Context/Activity
9.00	N	Elena	Arriving at centre
9.15	C	Henna, Elena	Digging in the sandpit
9.30	C	Henna, Elena	Digging in the sandpit
9.45	C	Henna, Emma, Jane	Hosing water – sandpit
10.00	C	Emma, Elena	Inside, at computer

C = Co-operative play – playing with other children, conversing together, borrowing or lending material, joint involvement in activity.
N = any activity/context other than C, including unoccupied.
Prepared as an example only. Adapted from Smith (1998: 62).

Time sampling

This approach is rather like interval recording, except that a particular behaviour is observed at the end of a short interval of time. As Anne Smith (1998: 61–2) notes:

> [Time sampling] is thus much easier to use when teaching, especially if the intervals are made to be relatively long (say, 20 minutes). For example, a teacher can observe a particular child at fifteen-minute intervals to see whether she is involved in co-operative behaviour, with whom, and in what activity.

As Smith explains, the extent of a child's co-operative behaviour can be documented through time sampling (as shown in Table 3.7).

An outside observer, or an observer released from teaching responsibilities and with more time available, can use shorter time intervals (around one minute).

Target child observations

Techniques of time sampling and coding of behaviour are incorporated within the target child method (Sylva *et al.* 1986). This was devised and first used for an observational study of 120 children aged between 3 and 5 in Oxfordshire, as part of the Oxford Pre-School Research Project, led by Jerome Bruner. It has been much used since, by students and researchers, and was one of the

Table 3.8 Target child observation template

Initials of TC:	Boy/girl	Age:	Date:	Time:
Activity	**Language**	**Task**		**Social**
1.				
2.				
3.				
4.				
5.				
6.				
7.				
8.				
9.				
10.				

Source: Based on Sylva *et al.* (1986: 231).

methodological tools used to observe children's learning in the Effective Provision of Pre-School Education (EPPE) project (Sylva *et al.* 2004). Designed for ease of data gathering, and common coding across a large sample, the observer uses a prepared template (see Table 3.8). The codes take a little time to learn, but once they are mastered a large amount of information can be recorded efficiently.[1]

Each section on the template represents one minute. In the 'activity' column the observer notes what the child is doing and any context, e.g. 'puzzle table, selection of jigsaws, TC tips pieces out of 12 piece fitting tray'. What the child says, and to whom, is noted in the language column, e.g. TC → C 'this is the farm one'; speech to the child is also noted, e.g. A →TC 'Oh, you chose the animal puzzle'. 'A' denotes adult and 'C' another child. If a child is involved in a particular activity or linked sequence of activities for several minutes then this becomes a theme. The observer draws double lines to show where one theme ends and another begins. This shows for how long play themes are sustained. The type of task is recorded – e.g. play with jigsaws would be coded as 'SM' for 'structured materials' – and also the presence of others. If the child was playing in parallel with others in a small group it could be coded 'SG/P', with this code circled to denote an adult's presence.

Checklists

Checklists are lists of specific behaviours that are of interest to the observer. They require the observer to use a coding sheet and, most often, to follow a process of ticking off specified behaviours each time they occur.

Checklists have several potential uses. For example, Anne Smith (1998: 63) explains that:

> Checklists can be applied periodically at different points in time to see who has reached the objectives in various points of a teaching programme. It is particularly valuable for developmental firsts to be recorded as they occur in young children. For infants in a childcare centre, for instance, the date and age at which individual children achieve certain skills such as crawling, standing alone, walking alone, single word sentences and the object concept can be recorded. ['Object concept' includes being able to match objects.]

In this way, using checklists has sometimes helped teachers and parents to communicate meaningfully about the progress of children with learning disabilities. On the whole, checklists have helped to focus the observations made by teachers, assessors and researchers.

Examples of detailed checklists developed internationally for early childhood research and practice include the *Portage Guide to Early Education* (Bluma *et al.* 1976) and the *Keele Preschool Assessment Guide* (Tyler 1979), see Table 3.9.

Checklists also have a number of limitations. They may have been used too often in early childhood settings, sometimes without adequate appraisal of their appropriateness. Fleer and Richardson (2004: 8) caution that:

> Compartmentalizing the image of the child engaged in a myriad of activities in the centre (observation) through carving up what is taking place into a physical box (analysis), frequently means that the texture of meaning surrounding the observation can be lost or rendered meaningless.

If you are planning to use a checklist as an observational tool, it is worthwhile reflecting on the extent to which it describes children holistically. Another consideration is whether its use will empower those who will be observed – the children, their families, or any other adults. This caution applies to all forms of observation.

Table 3.9 Items from a detailed checklist

This is part of the scoring sheet from the *Keele Preschool Assessment Guide* (Tyler 1979).
Note: This guide includes sets of items pertaining to cognition, physical skills, socialization and language. The examples set out below are from the language section of the guide.

Section 11
Read the items listed below and tick those which the child performs easily or frequently. (For definition of the items, refer to the manual.)

L1 Language use
☐ 1. Knows full name and a few nursery rhymes.
☐ 2. Able to relate experiences and knows several rhymes.
☐ 3. Can listen to and tell long stories.
☐ 4. Gives full name, sex, age, and address.
☐ 5. Able to hold lengthy conversations.

L2 Speech
☐ 1. Uses words other than nouns and verbs.
☐ 2. Uses pronouns, plurals, and past tense.
☐ 3. Uses complex sentence structures.
☐ 4. Uses passive structures and auxiliary verbs.
☐ 5. Frequently uses complex sentences with correct order of words.

L3 Vocabulary
☐ 1. Can name simple objects and identify parts of the body.
☐ 2. Can name colours and parts of the body.
☐ 3. Recognises own name when written.
☐ 4. Can name simple shapes and secondary colours.
☐ 5. Recognises some letters and simple words.

L4 Comprehension
☐ 1. Obeys simple commands and answers simple questions.
☐ 2. Can give definitions of simple words.
☐ 3. Comprehends stories and answers complex questions.
☐ 4. Obeys more complex instructions.
☐ 5. Can define differences between pairs of words.

A checklist can be used as a means of recording an analysis that summarizes a series of observations, rather than as the observational tool. Brief anecdotal observations of children's achievements can be recorded onto Post-it® notes and these small pieces of evidence can be used as a basis for completion of a checklist. In English early years settings, this approach is often used to track children's progess in each of the areas of learning within the EYFS curriculum (Luff 2012).

Table 3.10 Items from a simple rating scale

For each rating item, please circle the number that best indicates your observations:

1. This teacher responds to children with warmth and affection:

Strongly agree	Agree	Neutral	Disagree	Strongly disagree
1	2	3	4	5

2. This teacher allows children to make choices:

Strongly agree	Agree	Neutral	Disagree	Strongly disagree
1	2	3	4	5

Note: Constructed as a simple example. Rating scales ideally include full descriptions of the behaviour or characteristics rated (e.g. Laevers 1994).

Rating scales for early learning

Rating scales provide a way of using observations of children and adults to describe different levels of interaction. An example of a simple rating scale is set out in Table 3.10.

In early childhood settings and school classrooms, observations may be rated to assess levels of child and adult involvement or engagement. Involvement can be with people, tasks, or the environment. As in Table 3.10, this approach uses a scale with a number of points on it, usually a 4- or 5-point scale. Each point on the scale represents a specific, defined level. One potential disadvantage of rating scales is that they require a high level of judgement on the part of the observer, which can lead to inconsistency. For this reason, interobserver reliability is important. The rating scales and the related research studies summarized below, as examples, are generally associated with relatively high inter-rater reliability.

Involvement scale

The Leuven Involvement Scale for Young Children was developed in Belgium by Laevers (1994) to measure the quality of young children's experiences. This scale rates children's involvement on a 5-point scale (from level 1 = no activity, to level 5 = sustained, intense activity). It requires the observer to focus on and rate, at 2-minute intervals, the child's 'involvement signals'. The involvement signals include: concentration, energy, creativity, facial expressions and posture, persistence, precision, reaction time and language. The Leuven Involvement Scale for Young Children has been used in a range of early childhood education centres in Europe and the United Kingdom, in studies that report quite high inter-rater reliability (Pascal *et al*. 1994; Foster 1996).

Engagement scale

The Effective Early Learning (EEL) programme, developed by Chris Pascal and Tony Bertram in Worcester and Birmingham, is a self-evaluation programme for early childhood practitioners. The intention is to identify and reflect on good practice in centres, and to improve quality. The whole process takes about 9–12 months. There are four phases: Evaluation; Action Planning; Development; and Reflection (Pascal and Bertram 1997).

Two observation and rating techniques are used as a basis for evaluation:

- the Child Involvement Scale; and
- the Adult Engagement Scale.

The emphasis is on rating the level of involvement of children in their activities, and the level of engagement and effective teaching shown by adults (Pascal and Bertram 1997). These levels are measured in the evaluation phase. In the action planning and development phases strategies are devised and implemented, with the aim of increasing the quality of children's experiences. Levels are then measured again to assess the impact of changes and as a basis for further reflection and planning.

Like the EEL, the Baby Effective Early Learning (BEEL) programme includes interviews, documentary analysis and observations. The BEEL observations also focus on rating child and adult engagement.

Child engagement includes two aspects of infants' and toddlers' behaviours and experiences: connectedness, and exploring the environment. Connectedness means having a sense of location in the world. It includes infants' and toddlers' independence, openness, alertness, participation and friendliness. It is necessary for infants' and children's emotional wellbeing, and for effective learning. According to Pascal (2003: 23), connectedness can be seen (for example) in children's 'ability to relate to others, to interlink events and situations in their life and to feel part of the whole' and in their 'sense of attachment and belonging to the people with whom they come into close and regular contact, both adults and children'. When children explore their environment and make sense of it, they construct hypotheses and carry out purposeful exploration.

To rate child engagement, the scale describes three levels for each of the three key elements (i.e. connectedness, exploring the environment, and making sense of the environment). The adult engagement measure of BEEL is essentially the same instrument as EEL, but focuses more on involving parents.

Specific strengths of the Effective Early Learning observations and evaluations are:

- The Effective Early Learning (EEL) Professional Development/Research Project specifically outlines methods for including children's perspectives (Pascal *et al.* 1996).
- The process used in the EEL project is designed to be collaborative (working with the participants), and inclusive (appropriate for a range of early childhood settings). Chris Pascal (2003: 21) describes it this way: '... we embarked on a process of practical research and development. The process has involved us working closely in a range of early childhood settings with practitioners, children and families ...'.
- Pascal and Bertram recognize that early childhood settings are influenced by cultural norms and societal values, and they aim to capture the 'essence of quality' as reflected in practice, and to explore how this quality is perceived and experienced by the people involved (Pascal and Bertram 1997; Podmore and Meade 2000).

Environmental rating scales

Rating scales can also be used to evaluate the general environment of early childhood centres and services, across a diverse range of settings. Harms and Clifford, researchers in the United States, have provided a series of scales for this purpose. They first developed the Early Childhood Environment Rating Scale (ECERS) for rating the quality of early childhood environments in general (Harms and Clifford 1980). Their second instrument, the Family Day Care Rating Scale, is for rating family day-care settings and takes into account the special characteristics of home-based early childhood arrangements (Harms and Clifford 1989). In addition, they worked on further refinements to their initial scale to make it more suitable for rating the environments of centres that cater for infants, resulting in the publication of an Infant/Toddler Environment Rating Scale (Harms *et al.* 1990). A revised, updated version was published 18 years after their first scale (Harms *et al.* 1998).

Several research studies have used rating scales developed with reference to work by Harms and Clifford. An important UK example is the EPPE project (Sylva *et al.* 2004). This large-scale study, investigating the effects of pre-school education and care on children's development, used ECERS-R as a tool to study the characteristics and quality of participating early years settings. In order to assess specific aspects of educational provision, four additional subscales (ECERS-E) were devised in order to rate language, mathematics, science and the environment, and diversity. Significant links were shown between high-quality pre-school provision (as measured by ECERS ratings) and better intellectual and behavioural outcomes on entry to primary school.

Table 3.11 NZCER's Centre/Service Rating Scale (reported items)

Staff–child interaction
Staff are responsive.
Staff model and encourage redirection, positive reinforcement.
Staff guide children in the context of the centre.
Staff ask open-ended questions to encourage own responses.
Staff join children in their play.

Programme/activity focus
Children can select their own activities.
The centre is a 'print-saturated environment'.
Children work on social and maths/science problems and experiment.
Imaginative play.
Stories told.
Evidence of children's artwork and creativity.

Physical environment
Enough age-appropriate toys, etc.
Good safety procedures.
Equipment and activities encourage fine motor skills development.
Equipment and activities encourage gross motor skills development.
Easy access indoors to outdoors.

Self-esteem
Activities not sex-stereotyped.
Tikanga Māori evident.
Recognition of cultures.
Children co-operate and support one another.
Children allowed time to complete activities.

Source: Wylie *et al.* (2001: 76).

The Centre/Service Rating Scale of the New Zealand Council for Educational Research (NZCER) was adapted and developed during the first phases of the Competent Children study. It was used between October 1993 and August 1994 to evaluate 87 participating centres and services (Wylie *et al.* 1996). Although it has some scales that focus on environments, it attends much more to pedagogical practices.

The scale is divided into four subscales, each including various items. The subscales and key items (later also described by the researchers as 'quality indicators') are set out in Table 3.11.

As in most rating scales, including the Leuven Involvement Scale, a 5-level scale applies. Each of the separate items listed under each of the four subscales is rated from 1 ('never occurs, or not like this centre') to 5 ('always, or like this centre') (Wylie *et al.* 1996: 5).

The pilot study research report shows that the researchers checked precise guidelines carefully before they made decisions about their final ratings. The excerpt below gives an example of how the observational ratings were carried out:

> ... Throughout each visit to each ECS [education and care service], researchers carefully observed the environment, the programme, and the interactions between children and adults. A final rating for each variable was assigned at the end of the visit.
>
> Researchers referred to precise guidelines before making their final ratings. For example, when rating 'staff's responsiveness to children', researchers considered whether staff responded quickly, adapted their responses to children, their physical proximity to children, use of verbal encouragement, and so on. If researchers considered that staff always reacted to children in a highly responsive manner, the ECS was rated a '5'; if staff never reacted in this way, a rating of '1' was given, and so on.
>
> (Hendricks and Meade 1993: 60)

Findings from the Competent Children study show that children who had attended early childhood centres that were rated highly on certain items of NZCER's Centre/Service Rating Scale had a greater chance of being judged competent at mathematics and language when they were 10 years of age (when compared with children who had been at centres or services with lower ratings). Centre-quality 'items' that were linked to children's later competence at mathematics included (for example): 'staff guide children in the context of the centre', 'staff ask open-ended questions', 'children can select their own activities', and 'children allowed time to complete their activities' (Wylie *et al.* 2001: 76). The researchers gave this description of the overall influence of early childhood education on competencies at age 10 years:

> The long-lasting aspects of early childhood quality education are related to how teachers interact with children, and whether they interlace warmth with cognitive content, building on children's own interests ...
>
> (Wylie *et al.* 2001: 254)

Rating scales are useful when specific judgements, or external evaluations, are needed to summarize the observers' impressions. As in the Competent Children study and the EPPE project, they can be used appropriately as one of a wide selection of measures. In many circumstances and educational settings, however, a stronger emphasis on self-evaluation leads to empowering, participatory evaluation processes for practitioners. Further self-evaluation approaches are discussed in the next chapter.

Qualitative approaches

Qualitative observations use words and are usually richly descriptive. They are usually collectively called 'narratives' (although the word 'narrative' is sometimes more strictly applied only to 'storied' approaches like Learning Stories). The following sections of this chapter describe and discuss a range of qualitative approaches, with some examples provided.

Anecdotal or diary records

These narrative records describe excerpts or episodes of interactions that are recorded at different times in a child's or an adult's life. Anecdotal and diary records are written in the past tense, after the behaviour occurs, and usually show changes over time. Diary descriptions provide a personal account of children's and adults' experiences. They are written from the perspective of the writer of the diary entries, who may be the child's parent. Diary records usually include some samples of speech or interactions. They have been used to describe children's milestones and transitions. Some of the earliest examples of systematic diary records come from Charles Darwin's descriptions of his own child's behaviour (see Chapter 2).

A more recent example is Margery Renwick's (1997) research on New Zealand children's transition to school at the age of 5 years. As part of her study, Renwick asked mothers of children starting school to keep diary records of their children's experiences and of their own feelings about the transition. The excerpt in Table 3.12 shows what one mother wrote down the week before her child started going to school, on the first day the child attended school, and for the rest of the first week at school.

Diaries can provide vivid descriptions and explain children's and adults' personal experiences of events. However, the experiences recorded may be quite selective, unless they are supplemented by systematic observations. Diary descriptions are written subjectively and are likely to be from the single point of view of the person doing the recording.

Diaries and personal accounts of experiences were widely used by feminist researchers during the 1980s and 1990s to provide insights from women (Smith 1998). Diaries, often supplemented by detailed observations, are also increasingly used in research with children and students, to include the children's own perspectives. These may take the form of blogs or video diaries.

Running records or continuous recording

In general, a running record 'attempts to provide an account of what the child does from moment to moment, in a particular setting' (McMillan and Meade

Table 3.12 Parent's diary: Tom

The week before school

The week before Tom started school, we were on holiday, which probably meant he didn't
   think so much about it as he would have done if we were at home.

Tom said one day, 'You don't have to be scared at school, do you?' and later, 'It can be a fire
   at school but the teacher will take care of us.' I'm sure he was worried or thoughtful about
   starting school.

He went for three visits, which I found good. He got to know the teacher and he also realised
   that he knew most of the children from kindy. *[sic]*

The first day

Tom was quite keen to go and didn't seem nervous. We both went with him and the
   principal took us to the classroom. His best friend from kindy was waiting for him and he
   said bye bye to us after a few minutes.

It felt strange and a bit lonely to go home . . .

Rest of the week

Tom is happy to go every morning and doesn't seem to be that tired in the afternoon . . .

When I ask him what they have been doing during the day, he doesn't say a lot. 'A bit of
   everything.'

Source: Renwick (1997: 5).

1985: 8). Running records or continuous recordings can yield detailed descriptions of individual children's (or adults') behaviour or interactions for specific periods of time. The preparation of running records provides useful practice at recording observations accurately, with considerable detail, and with some attention to the immediate environment. Another strength of this technique is that continuous recordings are useful to document everything that takes place 'in situations where one wants to observe the totality of behaviour' (Smith 1998: 53).

One constraint of running records is that it can be difficult to write down everything that goes on for a child or adult continuously for about twenty minutes without being selective. This can be overcome to some extent by making an audio or video recording, as in the following example of a transcript of a 10-minute running record, but the transcription process that follows is time-consuming.

As in Table 3.13, running records or continuous recordings are written in the present tense, recording everything as it happens: e.g. 'A grabs a book . . .' The continuous 'narrative' of a running record may be structured, or coded, using specific events or categories, after the recording is completed. However, structuring and coding of running records like this one are carried out only

Table 3.13 A running record

This example of a thorough running record observation, prepared from a video recording, was provided by staff of the School of Early Childhood Teacher Education, College of Education, Victoria University of Wellington.

Child:	A
Date:	(day, month, year)
Time:	1.00–1.10 pm
Setting:	On the mat in book corner at the early childhood centre
Weather:	Wet and cold, raining
Age:	9 months

A is sitting on the floor with her legs wide apart, stomach and shoulders rounded, back straightish. She leans over to her left from the waist, bottom slightly raised, left leg tucked into her right leg. A grasps a book off the floor in her right hand, sits up straight again and tosses the book by flicking her wrist. She picks up the book again using thumb and all fingers, then drops it. A looks around the room, turning her head from the neck and says 'Dah.' She looks and then picks up book, grasps it in her left hand and says 'Dah dah.' A teacher is heard calling to another child so A looks up at her, sitting still. She lets go of the book by opening out her hand. Then A leans forward at waist, bottom on ground, stretches out her right arm and picks up the book, using her right hand thumb and all fingers grasped, then lets it go again onto the bean bag. She picks the book up again, looking at it, then watches a boy run across the floor, moving her head at the neck as she follows his movement. A looks back in front of her at the book, then she slips the book out of her hand by flapping her arm, moving from the shoulder. 'Dah dah,' she babbles, then she swaps the book into her other hand with her arms crossing over her body. She sucks her top lip in so her bottom lip sticks out, lets it go then looks up at a teacher standing nearby. A then looks back at the book and says 'Bab bab.' She leans over the waist onto her right leg and sort of giggles 'Ha, ha, ha, ha' while smiling broadly, she is leaning onto both arms stretched straight out in front of her palms flat on the floor. A pushes off the floor with her arms and sits, back straight. She picks up the book in her right hand using thumb and all fingers to grasp it, then drops it, picks it up in her left hand thumb and all fingers to grasp it, then drops it, picks it up in her left hand thumb and all fingers to grasp it and drops it. 'Bah Bah' she says then leans over to the left from the waist with her bottom just off the ground and leans on her left arm straight out, palm flat on the floor. She pushes up off her left arm so is sitting up again. A picks up the book again in her right hand and moves her arm around and puts the book down on her right side. Then A leans over onto her right leg using her right arm to hold herself up which is straight and the palm of her hand flat on the floor. She kicks out her left leg and foot then leans back saying 'Da da da.' A picks up the book in her right hand and passes it across her body. Then she picks up the book in her left hand, passes it back across her body into her right hand and puts it down on the outside of her right leg. A picks the book up again in her right hand,

Table 3.13 (*Continued*)

brings her left hand in to hold with both hands, fingers and thumb grasp, arms bent at the elbow and then she puts the flat side of the book to her face and opens her mouth. 'Hah hab hab' and then jiggles up and down off her bottom. A teacher says to her, 'What are you doing, A?' A looks up at her, head moving from the neck, and smiles at her. She looks back down at the book, then leans over to the left, bottom slightly off floor on the right side, supporting herself with her left arm which is straight out and her palm flat on the floor. A picks up the book in her right hand, right arm straight and sits up again and drops it, looks up and watches a boy playing, her head turning at the neck as she follows his movement. Then A picks up the book from in front of her with her left hand raises her arm slightly and drops it. A pats the book with the palm of her left hand, arm straight out, then she picks up the book again, using thumb and 4-finger grasp. She swings her left arm slowly around behind her, arm straight, moving from the shoulder, then she drops the book. She looks back at it over her shoulder, turning her head from the neck, upper body turned slightly at waist. With her left hand she picks it up again and swings her arm back around to her side and drops the book. A turns back to the front and grabs the bean bag in front of her in both hands and pulls it up to her mouth. She bites the bag and turns left slightly, from the waist to look at the teacher while still holding the bag with both hands gripping it and the bag still clenched in her mouth.

after observing the child on three to five separate occasions and on different observational days.

Every observation should include background details if it is to be useful over time and as part of a larger collection of data. This suggestion applies not only to running records, but also to most other types of observation. It is useful with each running record to include details about:

- who or what is being observed, for example vocalizations, responsive interactions, persistence, gestures;
- the ages of the children (participants) under observation (when appropriate);
- the date and time of observation;
- location;
- the number of children and adults present; and
- contextual information to set the scene (such as inside or outside, the nature of the place, and weather conditions).

An example of a recording sheet for a running record is provided in Table 3.14.

Table 3.14 Running records: observation sheet

Child:

Age:

Girl/boy:

Setting/Place:

Weather:

Number of children present:

Number of adults present:

Table 3.15 Observational excerpt from ethnographic research

Infants and toddlers in New Zealand childcare centres
7.35 am. The first child arrives. This is Angela, the only under 1-year-old in this centre at the moment. She arrives with her mother. The caregiver holds Angela while the mother chats to the caregiver. They are looking at and discussing some new mobiles that have been hung up in the room, the mother wondering where the centre bought them from. After 5 minutes the mother peers very closely at the baby's face and waves good-bye and then she repeats this one more time until she is in the doorway that leads outside. As she opens the door to leave Angela gives a brief cry. Angela stops crying the second the mother is out of sight.

Ethnography

Ethnographic studies aim to provide a 'picture' of what is going on over an extended period of time in a particular setting. In education, this may involve describing and analysing events and interactions within an early childhood centre or service, or in a classroom. Ethnographic studies often use narrative observations. The observer is likely to map out a plan of the centre environment, and to record narrative observations of interactions and discussions.

One example of this type of approach is our study of infants and toddlers (Podmore and Craig 1991), which as well as generating data using category observations (a quantitative approach), also included ethnography. The ethnographic research was qualitative and included narrative observations, a map of the premises and interviews. A brief excerpt from the qualitative observations, focused on arrival and departure times, is set out in Table 3.15. This excerpt was cited in the research report as an example of the theme 'communication with parents'.

Another example of an ethnographic study from early childhood is Alison Stephenson's (1999) in-depth research on young children's outdoor experiences in a centre. Stephenson observed the children's interactions and environment repeatedly over a two-month period, prepared an inventory of the outdoor equipment, and later took numerous photographs. The short excerpt in Table 3.16 is one example of her observations that showed a 1-year-old child 'determined to get outside'.

Stephenson (1999: 3) reflected upon her choice of method:

This approach seemed particularly promising in a research situation where very little research-based knowledge existed. I also hoped that an ethnographic approach would diminish the gap between me, as researcher, and the practitioners in the centre. The process of observing, recording and reflecting is a key aspect of practitioners' role so I expected that there would be overlap in the methods we used, and we would share the same broad focus – increasing our understanding of the children.

A similar rationale influenced a decision to use ethnographic methods of observation in order to explore early years practitioners' understandings and uses of child observation during their first year in the workplace (Luff 2010).

Table 3.16 Opening up the outdoors: extract from ethnographic research

A case study of young children's outdoor experiences in one childcare centre
Early one very cold winter morning I watched Leo, wearing his gumboots which he had pulled on himself, go to the sliding door. This was being kept shut to prevent younger children from going outside. I noted:
Joanna goes outside, sliding the door open and shutting it after her. Leo watches. Emma and Pauline . . . come in and shut the door after them. Leo is standing by the door, boot on the glass, shouting but not loudly. Sara is outside and when Leo tries to go out, she picks him up: 'It's a bit cold for you, sweetie.' She puts him inside and slides the door shut. Leo begins to cry in a half-hearted way. He picks up a woolly hat out of the hat box. An adult puts him in the high chair for morning tea.
He had done all within his power to get outside but was frustrated, first by his inability to slide the door, and then when there was a gap, by the concerned adult. For most of the day both the indoor and outdoor environments were available to all children, and staff understood the frustration of these younger children when, for their own health and well-being, they were occasionally restricted to the inside.

Narratives

Narrative observations are recorded using words, often supplemented with visual material such as photographs, video clips and DVDs (Forman and Hall 2005; Collins *et al.* 2010). Narratives tend to emphasize the importance of infants' and young children's understanding, and their relationships with people, places and activities. Narrative or storied approaches in observations, as used in education settings, usually include reflections on the context and the cultural aspects of learning (Bruner 1990, 1996; Rogoff *et al.* 1993). Examples of these methods and their uses are given in the next chapter.

Summary

This chapter has described and appraised some key quantitative, followed by key qualitative, approaches to observation. The chapter illustrates a more recent shift to qualitative, sociocultural observations in early childhood educational settings. This is further explored in Chapter 4.

Note

1   For a full list of codes, see Sylva *et al.* (1986).

4 Processes – Learning and Teaching Stories

This chapter describes and discusses the importance of observation as a means of developing curriculum and assessing and evaluating learning. The Learning Stories approach, the dominant tool of assessment in use in early childhood centres in New Zealand, is described and its relevance for UK practitioners is highlighted. Teaching Stories are explained and considered as a self-evaluation strategy for enhancing the quality of early childhood provision. Practical sociocultural approaches to observation and assessment are explored.

Observational assessment in UK early years settings

The early years curricula of all four nations of the United Kingdom place emphasis upon the use of observation for curriculum planning and assessment (see Chapter 1). It is a requirement within the EYFS (DfES 2007) to undertake observations of children, engaged in a range of activities, and to use these observations to make judgements about children's progress and create further opportunities for learning. In Northern Ireland, Scotland and Wales, too, observation of children is key to the successful delivery of the curriculum.

There is no single format for documenting observations. In many early childhood settings each child has a personal portfolio in which written observations, art work and photographs are contained. This portfolio is sometimes referred to as a record of the child's 'Learning Journey'. The term 'Learning Journey' is also used to refer to an observation recorded using the Learning Journey template, included as a resource in the EYFS curriculum pack (DfES 2007). This template includes sections for evidence of the child's achievement, links to the EYFS areas of learning and development, the child's comments, practitioner reflections and ideas for follow-up activities (for examples see Collins *et al.* 2010; Papatheodorou *et al.* 2011). The metaphor of a learning 'journey' captures some of the adventure of early learning and also of distance travelled and destinations reached. It is important to have a sense of direction for children's learning but there is a risk that the mapping of the next steps along the path in a linear way may limit opportunities. A learning 'story' metaphor is also attractive, offering many possibilities for originality, sequels, new departures and negotiated directions. As Sally Peters (2009: 28) notes, 'stories about a person have the power to contribute to that person's narrative about themselves and about others'.

Another reason that educators in the UK have begun to look at and to use a Learning Stories approach is a shared interest in the importance of learning dispositions (e.g. Katz 1988; Carr 2001; Claxton and Carr 2004). Learning dispositions can be defined as 'habits of mind, tendencies to respond to situations in certain ways' (Katz 1988: 30). Positive learning dispositions reflect qualities that equip learners to respond to a variety of opportunities with enthusiasm and confidence. Learning dispositions and attitudes are included in a strand within the EYFS with the intention that children should 'continue to be interested, excited and motivated to learn' (DfES 2007: 25). A Learning Story approach to assessment can assist educators with understanding and planning for children's interests in order to create an environment that fosters curiosity, self-confidence and persistence with tasks.

Learning Stories

The Learning Stories framework was developed from Margaret Carr's (2001) ground-breaking research. It is underpinned by the four principles of *Te Whāriki* (New Zealand's bicultural early childhood curriculum): empowerment/*whakamana*; holistic development/*kotahitanga*; family and community/ *whānau tangata*; and relationships/*ngā hononga*. The Learning Stories framework is a set of five broadly based behaviours (or 'domains of disposition'; Carr, 2001: 177) linked to each of the five strands of *Te Whāriki* (see Introduction and Table 4.1).

Learning Stories are described as:

> Structured narratives that track children's strengths and interests: they emphasize the aim of early childhood as the development of children's identities as competent learners in a range of different arenas. They include an analysis of the learning (a 'short-term review') and a 'what next?' section. The narratives frequently include the interactions between teacher and learner, or between peers; often the episode is dictated by the learner as a 'child's voice'. The portfolios or folders in which they are housed invite families to contribute their own stories and comments.
>
> (Cowie and Carr 2009: 107)

The five key learning dispositions, together with the observable actions associated with them, are set out in Table 4.1.

Table 4.1 Key learning dispositions

Strand of *Te Whāriki*	Domain of learning disposition	Observable action
Belonging	(i) **Courage** and **curiosity** to find an interest here	Taking an interest
Well-being	(ii) **Trust** that this is a safe place to be involved and the **playfulness** that often follows from deep involvement	Being involved
Exploration	(iii) **Perseverance** to tackle and persist with difficulty or uncertainty	Persisting with difficulty, challenge and uncertainty
Communication	(iv) **Confidence** to express ideas or a point of view	Expressing a point of view or feeling
Contribution	(v) **Responsibility** for justice and fairness and the disposition to take another point of view	Taking responsibility

Source: Podmore *et al.* (2001: 7).

The narrative observations made to document Learning Stories are structured around the five key dispositions. Learning dispositions, as observable actions, have been defined as 'participation repertoires from which a learner recognizes, selects, edits, responds to, resists, searches for and constructs learning opportunities' (Carr 2001: 10). The observations are made over time to document progress. The Learning Stories format includes a basic form for recording Learning Story observations (see Table 6.1) as well as forms for recording the child's voice and the parents' voices. After these forms were developed and published, many teachers developed their own formats and used digital technology to include images in their documented Learning Stories. There are examples in Margaret Carr's (2001) book and in the *Kei Tua o te Pae/Assessment for Learning: Early Childhood Exemplars*, published by the New Zealand Ministry of Education (2009) and available on their website.

Learning Stories are connected to the sociocultural curriculum of *Te Whāriki*. In developing the Learning Stories approach, Margaret Carr described the learner as 'a learner in action'. Like Barbara Rogoff, she believes that 'development and learning are about transformation of participation', with the five features of participation being: taking an interest; becoming involved; persisting with difficulty, challenge and uncertainty; expressing a point of view; and taking responsibility (Carr 2001: 176). The main theoretical underpinning of a

Learning Stories approach to observation is, therefore, a sociocultural position on participation – with, for example, the inclusion of dispositions.

A completed example of a published Learning Story (Hedges 2003: 5–6), focused on a child who is learning scientific concepts, is presented here as Table 4.2.

Learning Stories are an innovative way of assessing children's learning. Their strong focus on children's strengths and interests means that they are credit-based. The affirmation of their abilities, as displayed and celebrated in the Learning Story, helps children to build up strong positive identities of themselves as learners (Drummond 1993; Carr 2001; Peters 2009). The Learning Story records something that the child has worked on and achieved, like Hayden's understanding of the relationship between magnetism and materials made from metal (see example). For practitioners working within the EYFS framework, in addition to evidence of interest, excitement and motivation to learn, this could be noted as an example of using language for thinking and of achievement within the exploration and investigation aspect of the knowledge and understanding of the world area of learning (DfES 2007).

Learning Stories also provide a tool for identifying interests and planning the next steps in a child's learning, in order to provide personalized active learning experiences. As Caryl Hamer (1999: 66) has noted: 'A focus on what the child can do allows educators to identify effective and appropriate strategies for further progress and learning.' By using narrative, the Learning Stories approach allows for recognition of, reflection on, and responses to the complexity of learning. In Hayden's case, teachers have to consider their own scientific subject knowledge as well as making judgements about future opportunities for experimentation to reinforce and extend Hayden's developing concept knowledge.

The response of early childhood teachers and parents to the Learning Stories approach to observation, assessment and documentation has been overwhelmingly positive (Carr 2001; Peters 2009). It is often a challenge for practitioners to include the voices of children and parents. Learning Stories allow for the child's view and parents' perspectives to be heard and included in assessment. Peters (2009) argues that a Learning Story approach can play an important part in fostering responsive and reciprocal relationships through the sharing of information it promotes with parents and families, who become more a part of the early childhood centre community as a result.

One possible constraint relates to time and training. Professional development is needed, and sufficient time and commitment are necessary for early childhood teachers to implement Learning Story observations effectively. There have been questions, too, about the emphasis of Learning Stories on the individual child (Fleer 2002). However, Learning Stories are about active participation in learning in the group and in the community. Bronwen Cowie and Margaret

Table 4.2 A Learning Story

Hayden explores theories about the properties of a magnet.

Hayden has indicated earlier an interest in and knowledge about cars, e.g. 'I know all of the cars' names' . . .

Penguin 3 takes a Cherokee, eh Penguin 3? (no response) And I know what your car's called, your little one, a white one . . . . I know Mary's car, I know your car – a Rover. Idiot! – He was driving way too fast up the street, must be a two-litre one . . .'

Links to *Te Whāriki* curriculum	Learning Story record
Belonging/*mana whenua* – taking an interest – the child's interest was in the magnet. His inquiry was linked by the adult to another interest of his – cars. Prior knowledge of children is a key feature of sociocultural approaches to curriculum and pedagogy.	Towards the end of group time, Hayden approaches me on the deck and shows me a small round magnet he has found. He tells me he found it on the ground and that it sticks to things. I ask him what sort of things and he replies 'dark things'. I suggest we go and see if there is anything it will stick to in the kitchen. He successfully tries the fridge and the dishwasher. I ask him whether they are dark and he replies, 'no, white'.
Well-being/*mana atua* – being involved – the child paid attention to and concentrated on inquiry into and discovering the properties of magnets for a sustained period of time with an adult. He was playful with a variety of equipment to test his theories.	I ask him what he thinks the doors of the fridge and the dishwasher are made of and he frowns, 'I don't know'. He discovers the magnet attaches to the doorframe, then the stapler in the collage area. He stops to think and says to me 'Let's go outside and find a hammer'. He runs to the carpentry area and tests out his theory. 'Yes! Let's try a saw!' He quickly finds several other things on the carpentry trolley and joints on the trolley itself that the magnet attaches to. I ask him again what these things are made of, and suggest it may be the same material as cars. His face brightens in realization 'Let's see what else is metal at kindy!' and runs to the climbing frame. 'Come, look!' as he finds several items the magnet attaches to.
Exploration – *mana aotūroa* – persisting with difficulty – the child was confused about the (metal – aluminium) ladder but continued testing his theory on other materials that he considered fitted his theory.	
Communication – *mana reo* – expressing an idea or a feeling – the child communicated his interest, theories, investigation, puzzlement and understanding verbally and non-verbally.	
Contribution – *mana tangata* – taking responsibility – the child responded to the experience and new learning by showing another child what to do and discussing his knowledge and theories.	

(Continued)

Table 4.2 (*Continued*)

Links to *Te Whāriki* curriculum	Learning Story record
	Helen: 'How does a magnet work?' Hayden: 'I don't know, let's look for some more metal.' He runs to the ladder, but the magnet falls off. He theorizes 'It must be too wet' and tries again. It still falls off. He theorizes 'maybe it's not metal' (it is aluminium). He finds the chain around the tyres under the fort, the joints of the fort, nails on the wooden frame, runs to the guinea pig cage and tries the metal on that, then runs to the fence. He calls to me 'Come, look!' I catch up, writing notes furiously, and he says, 'Let's find some more metal' and runs to the water trough. I suggest he tries the chairs. He runs over and tests the legs of the chairs rather than the plastic seats. 'Yes, it works.' He then runs back to the carpentry trolley and checks the legs of that. 'Ooh, look, that works!' Helen: 'What do you think makes it stick?' Hayden: 'I don't know.' Helen: 'Shall we find a book about magnets?' Hayden runs inside to the container of books and we find a book about magnets. We read about 'poles', 'force', and 'pull'. There are pictures of objects for children to theorize whether or not magnets will stick to them. Hayden immediately points to the car and says magnets will stick to them because they are metal. We return to the kitchen to see if we can feel the 'pull' of the magnet on the fridge. I ask him if the magnet is hard to pull off and he responds 'yes'. Jamie has joined us and asks if she can have a turn. He passes the magnet to her and she tries to put it on the fridge the wrong way round and it falls down. Hayden picks it up and shows her how it works. Jamie tries the magnets that are on the fridge and comments 'These are easier'. Helen: 'So which has the strongest pull?' Jamie: 'Hayden's.' Helen: 'Why do you think that might be?' Hayden: 'We didn't try this' – and tries the corner of the kitchen bench.

Table 4.2 *(Continued)*

Links to *Te Whāriki curriculum*	Learning Story record
	The magnet falls off. 'Hey! I thought this was metal!' Another child joins us and asks Hayden to go and play with him. Hayden does so.

What next?

A focus on the dispositions of 'being a scientist' and 'thinking scientifically'. Incorporate *Te Whāriki*, 'exploration' goals three and four and link to Science in the New Zealand Curriculum, level one.

- Offer different types and strengths of magnets to differentiate between, e.g. bar magnets, horseshoe magnets.
- Experiment with magnetic attraction between an item on a table, e.g. paper clips and the magnet underneath the table.
- Walk to the beach or get some beach sand that contains iron sand to use with magnets. Only sand from the west coast beaches contains iron.
- Use iron filings with the magnets.
- Demonstrate the use of a compass. Plan an 'orienteering' expedition.
- Offer learning experiences with other kinds of forces, e.g. static electricity.

What subject knowledge might a teacher need to guide children's thinking about magnets?

A force is an invisible push or pull that makes a person or object move, stop, or alter speed or direction. Some forces are direct contact (e.g. a rolling pin on playdough, or pushing a wooden truck or swing) and others occur when two objects are not in direct contact (e.g. magnets).

Iron, nickel and cobalt are the metals that can be magnetized.

Steel is predominantly iron and so steel objects can be magnetized too. Other metals (e.g. gold, silver, copper, aluminium, lead, chromium) and alloys (brass, bronze, pewter which are mixtures of different metals) will not attract magnets. Sometimes a thin plating of a non-magnetic metal such as chromium will cover iron (for example on taps) and the magnet will stick. In these cases the magnetic force extends through the surface layer in the same way that magnets can 'work' from under a wooden table to move metal objects on top of the table.

- Earth has a magnetic force field related to its poles (North and South). A compass demonstrates how the magnetic needle always points north. Magnets have two strong places at opposite ends of the magnet. These are also called poles. Poles of the same kind push each other away; poles of a different kind pull towards each other. When metals that can be magnetized come into a magnetic force field, their particles become temporarily polarized and they behave as if they are magnets too. In most cases this effect disappears as soon as the magnet is moved away but some types of steel will remain magnetized if touched with a sufficiently strong magnet – at least for a while.

Table 4.2 (*Continued*)

Links to *Te Whariki* curriculum	Learning Story record
	There are several other types of forces, e.g.
	• The planet Earth has a 'force' that tries to pull everything towards its centre. This is called 'gravity'. This force means that when we throw something up in the air, it will land back on the ground. The moon's gravitational forces are seen in daily tidal flows and patterns of the seas on Earth.

Note: More information and ideas for exploring metals with young children can be found in the *Building Science Concepts* series: Book 32, *Introducing Metals* (Learning Media 2003)

Carr (2009: 97) describe how 'the community may have a strong voice in the interpretation of such aims as "belonging", "contribution", and "communication"'. They explain that the Learning Story approach, like *Te Whāriki* itself, leaves scope for local 'weaving', local interpretation, and being locally legitimated. It is this flexibility that makes it transferable to UK contexts (Coates and Thomson 2010).

Teaching Stories

Teaching Stories is a related narrative approach, developed in New Zealand, for teachers to evaluate their own practice. Learning Stories can form a basis for professional dialogues about children's learning and how it can be facilitated. Teaching Stories go further and prompt reflections upon the systems, structures and processes put in place by teachers and practitioners as part of ongoing evaluation and accountability procedures.

This approach to teachers' self-evaluation was developed from observations carried out as part of an ethnographic research study (May and Podmore 2000), see Table 4.4. Learning Stories and Teaching Stories are closely connected. The Teaching Story framework emerged from the five behaviours in the Learning Story framework. An example of one of the first Teaching Stories that was developed from observations, by a researcher/observer in consultation with the teacher, is shown here as Table 4.3. The Teaching Story reveals what the educator is doing to promote the learning dispositions that are valued in the children.

The 'Child's Questions' have become an integral part of the Teaching Stories approach. There are five Child's Questions, each linked to a strand of *Te Whāriki* and a learning disposition. Their purpose is for teachers to reflect on and monitor their own teaching interactions with children, from children's

Table 4.3 Early example of a Teaching Story

This is a Teaching Story developed for research purposes, from observations.

Adult J's Teaching Story

Early one morning as the children arrive

Belonging	J is focused on ensuring that each parent and child is given a special time as they arrive. Their needs are varied and J responds to each differently. There are many conversational connections made between home and kindergarten and J attempts to use 'home' connections as a lead into something the child might like to explore or do in the kindergarten. At this time the parents are given 'equal' attention with the children. Some of this attention relates to the children, but some is specific to the adult.
Well-being	The children's main needs at this early time are being made to feel welcome, and for J to acknowledge that what they want to show or tell is interesting or relevant. J allows time for children to feel settled and looks for ways to facilitate parents leaving their child and then for the child to feel that they can move beyond J. The pattern is different for every child. For one or two children this is a longer process. But in time J settles all the children. Many however have confidently said hello and settled themselves into some play activity. J responds promptly to requests from children although not necessarily solving the 'problem' herself.
Exploration	As the children settle J moves first to the dough table where she plays with dough herself to encourage one child in particular that this is a possible place to play. From this observation it is clear that children will not move towards 'exploratory' activities until they have a sense of well-being and belonging. In the collage area J follows children's interests and agenda to support, facilitate and extend their ideas. Children were encouraged to keep thinking about what they were doing and the children were staying in the task for a period of time. The children's needs were very different and it was a matter of continually connecting with what a child had said or done previously – even on another day. J sometimes anticipates what a child might need to prevent frustration.
Communication	Ongoing verbal communication with individual children and parents. Encouraging children to respond to welcomes. Later J moves into group situation and verbal communication encompasses several children. Notices body languages of children and responds to many non-verbal cues during settling in time.
Contribution	Facilitating goodbyes between children and parents. Enabling children to feel they can choose what they might want to do themselves. Encouraging children to assist others or note what others are doing.

Source: Podmore and May (1998: 31).

Table 4.4 Excerpt from observational transcript

Adult J, Head Teacher, at arrival time during a morning kindergarten session.
9 am
J is sitting on the floor greeting children and parents as they arrive. One child arrives with a
    beautiful scarf. J asks to feel it and then admires child's glitter shoes. Mother says that she
    has given up and that she can wear what she wants. J responds that it is probably the best
    way. Child moves off.
Parent comes in who is on the committee and talks about an order to be dealt with. J then
    remarks to the child of this mother, who comes in with a box, 'What have you brought? Is
    it empty or is there something in it?'
Child acknowledges response with eyes but moves on to other children with box . . .

Source: Podmore and May (1998: 31–4).
Note: In the research report, three more pages of observational transcript follow. These are the
continuing observational records of 'arrival time' at the kindergarten. Adult J's Teaching Story above is
based on all of these observations.

perspectives. The full and simplified forms of the Child's Questions are set out in
Table 4.5.

An action research project (Carr *et al.* 2000; Podmore *et al.* 2001) developed a
number of action research tools (ARTs), based on these questions. These provide
examples of observation strategies for Teaching Stories. They were developed
and trialled at different types of early childhood centre by teachers and other
adults, working alongside an action research facilitator, and were judged to
be effective. An important aspect of the role of UK practitioners is to observe

Table 4.5 The Child's Questions

Strand of Te Whāriki	Full question	Simplified question
Belonging	Do you appreciate and understand my interests and abilities and those of my family?	Do you know me?
Well-being	Do you meet my daily needs with care and sensitive consideration?	Can I trust you?
Exploration	Do you engage my mind, offer challenges and extend my world?	Do you let me fly?
Communication	Do you invite me to communicate and respond to my own particular efforts?	Do you hear me?
Contribution	Do you encourage and facilitate my endeavours to be part of the wider group?	Is this place fair for us?

Source: Podmore *et al.* (2001: 7).

and reflect upon the children's play and the environment provided for care and learning. The Teaching Story examples and exercise, shown below, offer possible tools for reflective practice. The observation strategies in the following examples were judged effective for self-evaluation in early childhood centres because, on the whole, they are:

- capable of surprise, challenging assumptions;
- precise;
- capable of being analysed;
- linked to the child's question in a transparent way;
- quick and easy to use;
- suitable for starting analysis and planning processes in a short time-frame;
- capable of showing that action made a difference; and
- capable of energizing teachers/adults to reflect on their practice.

(Carr *et al.* 2000: 51–3)

In the first example (Table 4.6), observations are focused on the Wellbeing strand of *Te Whāriki* and the Child's Question is: 'Can I trust you?' Observation initially involves self-monitoring and reflection, and then in a second stage

Table 4.6 Teaching Stories: Can I trust you?

Strand of *Te Whāriki*: Well-being

Child's Question: Can I trust you?
(Do you meet my daily needs with care and sensitive consideration?)

Self-reflection on two episodes, followed by peer reflection.

Process: Self-observation and reflection (first level of difficulty)

Teachers/adults collect information on two episodes of their own interactions with children, where:
1. they respond to a child/children successfully in a sensitive manner; and
2. they feel they 'missed the boat' in responding to the child's mood or agenda.

This 'self-observation' needs to be recorded as soon as possible after the event.

Peer exercise (second level of difficulty)
A teacher/adult observes a peer (with his/her prior agreement), noting where:
1. the adult responds to a child/children successfully in a sensitive manner; and
2. she/he feels the adult 'missed the boat' in responding to the child's mood or agenda.

Note: Using this tool leads to self-reflection, and may encourage good relationships and honest sharing.

Source: Adapted from Carr *et al.* (2000: 86–7).

Table 4.7 Teaching Stories: Do you let me fly?

Strand of *Te Whāriki*: Exploration

Child's Question: Do you let me fly?
(Do you engage my mind, offer challenges and extend my world?)

The focus is on a particular context or area of the centre. The observer identifies
opportunities for children to 'extend their world'.

Process: Observation and reflection

Teachers/adults observe a selected context (or area of play) and record observations for a
specified period of time. Observations may be recorded on video.
Teachers/adults:

- collect examples where children tackle difficulty or challenge;
- collect examples where children avoid difficulty or challenge;
- collect examples where children persist with difficulty or challenge;
- collect examples where children give up; and
- note contributing environmental factors.

The team then share examples and reflections.

Note: Using this tool leads to self-reflection, and may lead to adults responsively offering
more challenges to children.

Source: Adapted from Carr *et al.* (2000: 51, 87).

moves on to a situation where peers (teachers) are observing one another. These
exercises would be useful for a key person to use as a basis for evaluating the
quality of relationship that she/he has with her/his key children.

The second example of an observation tool (Table 4.7) is connected to
the Exploration strand of *Te Whāriki* and to the Child's Question: 'Do
you let me fly?' The links with dispositions for learning are very clear
in this example. For UK practitioners, team discussion of observations of
an area of play could support the provision of stimulating experiences to
ensure that suitable physical and intellectual challenges are presented to
children.

The EYFS emphasizes the importance of active listening to children and it
is stated in the practice guidance that all children should be listened to and
respected (DfES 2007). Exercises like those in the next example may stimulate
reflection on effective listening to children and the support offered for communication. Table 4.8 involves two related tools: self-observation and reflection,
and peer observation. Observations are focused on Communication and the
Child's Question: 'Do you hear me?'

Table 4.8 Teaching Stories: Do you hear me?

Strand of *Te Whāriki*: Communication

Child's Question: Do you hear me?
(Do you invite me to communicate and respond to my own particular efforts?)

Process: Observation and reflection

Conversations are recorded on a chart as they occur. The observations are then collated and
   discussed at a staff/team meeting.

Teaching Stories: An example of an observation tool – 'Secret spies'

Strand of *Te Whāriki*: Communication

Child's question: Do you hear me?
(Do you invite me to communicate and respond to my own particular efforts?)

Process
Each staff person observes another (arranged with mutual consent). The observation focuses
   on what the adult does well to support children 'being heard'. Observations note
   specific episodes that illustrate the ways in which each person:
• listens to children;
• engages them in conversation; and
• responds to their efforts.

Note: Using this tool leads to self-reflection and, in a supportive environment, may enhance
the practice of listening carefully and responding reciprocally and respectfully to children.

Source: Adapted from Carr *et al.* (2000: 88).

The final example (Table 4.9) concerns Contribution and the Child's Question: 'Is this place fair for us?' Observation is focused on episodes of inclusion and exclusion and could form the basis for considering whether children have equal opportunities within a setting and how children's rights are upheld.

In general, effective observation tools for developing Teaching Stories:

• generate reflective discussion: they challenge assumptions, do not 'put staff down', and they make sense;
• are easily accessible and provide easily read evaluations: they may translate into a chart;
• speak to the interests of the teachers, adults and community;
• include teachers' peer observations of each other in an atmosphere of trust; and
• include early discussions and agreement about the criteria involved.

(Carr *et al.* 2000)

Table 4.9 Teaching Stories: Is this place fair for us?

Strand of *Te Whāriki:* Contribution

Child's Question: Is this place fair for us?
(Do you encourage and facilitate my endeavours to be part of the wider group?)

Process: Observation and reflection

Over a period of time, teachers/adults note all:

- incidents of children positively assisting other children and/or including them in the group; and
- incidents of excluding or of negative peer interactions. The observer also notes what were the contributing factors/the antecedents.

Note: Contexts within an educational setting, or areas of play, can be videotaped and later analysed with a focus on these incidents. Using this tool can lead teachers to 'reflect on their philosophy (teaching story) about fairness and what it [means] within their learning and teaching context'.

Source: Adapted from Carr *et al.* (2000: 42, 90).

A Teaching Story approach, as described above, could be very useful for creating and sustaining a culture of reflection and self-evaluation within UK settings. Observations using the environmental rating scales (see Chapter 3) can also be used to audit provision and plan improvement. Shared staff development work, using observational tools, shows that curriculum provision for children can be enhanced when it goes beyond individual practitioners planning for individual children and becomes, instead, a co-operative endeavour.

Sociocultural approaches to observations and planning

In contrast to the emphasis of the child-study movement on the individual child (see Chapters 1 and 2), there has been a move among early childhood researchers and teacher educators towards group observation and analysis (Fleer and Richardson 2004, 2009; Jordan 2009).

In Reggio Emilia the view of the child, first expressed by Loris Malaguzzi, is as 'rich in potential, strong, powerful, competent and most of all connected to adults and other children' (cited in Dahlberg *et al.* 1999: 50). In the preschools of Reggio Emilia, the role of the observant adult is to listen actively and make sense of what children are saying and doing in order to promote their competence in making and expressing meanings, through actively promoting the development of projects (*progettazione*). This is a complex task as it involves making sense of multiple viewpoints and supporting children to do this too. Tape recordings, photographs and video, and note taking are all part of this process, capturing the 'languages' of the children and providing documentation to make the learning visible. Decisions are made, on the basis of this looking and listening, about the resources, techniques and suggestions to be offered to the children as each project progresses. The documentation also serves to display the learning process to others and to allow children to revisit and reflect upon their learning (Rinaldi 2006).

The 'documenting in relationship with others' (Moss 2005: 27) that occurs in the *progettazione* in Reggio Emilia exemplifies a sharing of understandings in which children and educators create and capture educational experiences. The approach to early childhood pedagogy in Reggio Emilia has provided inspiration for other programmes, in different cultural contexts, which feature both children and adults learning in collaboration via the preparation and discussion of documentation. An example from the UK is the arts based *5x5x5=Creativity* project (Bancroft *et al.* 2008) in which artists work with schools and early years settings and in collaboration with cultural organizations (such as museums and galleries). The adults view themselves as 'researching the children researching the world' (Fawcett 2009: 133). They engage in cycles of observation, planning, action and reflection, using careful documentation of the activities as a basis for fostering and supporting creative processes.

In Sweden, early childhood institutions involved in the Stockholm Project (Dahlberg *et al.* 1999) worked on observation and pedagogical documentation, moving away from observing and recording designed to assess and classify individual children. The alternative was to 'swim in observations' (Dahlberg *et al.* 1999: 135) in order to examine and critique pedagogy and understand children's explorations and co-constructions of their world. This is well illustrated by the example of teacher Anna's experience of documenting what was said and done during a project about time (Dahlberg *et al.* 1999). Analysing her documented observations alone, with the children and with parents and colleagues, gave her the confidence to make pedagogical judgements, ask relevant questions and encourage the children's meaning making.

Marilyn Fleer and Carmel Richardson (2004, 2009) have developed a socio-cultural approach to documenting children's learning that focuses on children in a community of learners. Instead of observing and recording individuals, they propose ways of recording for groups of children:

> In Australia, we need to move beyond the microscopic, reductionist perspective on making observations of children. We now want and need the big picture in our observations. We need to move beyond focusing on the individual child. We want and need a mosaic of

observations – not just one child, but also a series of observations of small groups of children. We can always analyse these observations to find out about individuals ... Clearly, though, learning is not simply an individual construction.

(Fleer and Richardson 2004: 11)

Drawing on both Vygotsky's theoretical concept of the zone of proximal development and sociocultural ideas about co-construction, they suggest that child profiles might include columns to record what the child does 'with adult/peer support and minimal child input (modelled)', what is 'jointly undertaken by child and adult/peer (shared)', and whether the child 'takes leadership and/or works independently (independent)' (Fleer and Richardson 2004: 21). Fleer and Richardson (2009) also propose, in line with Barbara Rogoff's work on planes of analysis, an approach using three different 'lenses' (or ways of viewing) when observing and analysing. These lenses are:

- the personal (individual);
- the interpersonal (interactions between people); and
- the cultural (including cultural values and context).

They suggest how early childhood teachers can plan their programmes, by moving from a personal lens (focusing on individual children) to include interpersonal planning (with active planning for interactions among participants) and an institutional cultural lens (for questioning the cultural relevance, acceptability and appropriateness of materials, practices and routines for groups of children).

An advantage of a sociocultural approach to observation and assessment is that teaching interactions and co-construction are included in the observational records and notes. Sociocultural observations are in tune with and sensitive to the cultural context (Fleer and Richardson 2004, 2009; Rogoff 2003). One constraint is that, as Fleer and Richardson (2009) themselves note, it takes time for teaching staff to move from an individual focus on one child to a sociocultural approach. Teachers who participated in their research found that moving from an individual focus to a collective view and a sociocultural perspective was the most difficult part. As in the Learning Stories approach to observation and assessment and the Teaching Stories approach to self-evaluation, teacher education and qualifications, and continuing professional development, are important priorities when embarking on these approaches to observation.

Summary

This chapter has explained and explored Learning Stories and Teaching Stories, describing their uses in early childhood education in New Zealand and considering their relevance for practice in the UK. The influence of Reggio Emilia and approaches to observation in Australia illustrate a trend towards sociocultural understandings of observation. The next two chapters (5 and 6) are particularly concerned with observing for research purposes. Chapter 5 focuses on ethical issues to consider before starting any observational research.

Part III

Observation as research

5 Ethics

This chapter is particularly important when observing for research purposes. It defines ethics and examines the ethics of observing. The aim is to foster David Flinders's (1992) notion of 'ethical literacy' by addressing some ethical dilemmas. A further framework for research, developed by Joy Cullen, Helen Hedges and Jane Bone (2005, 2009), provides a useful guide to ethical issues when observing young children. The chapter includes suggestions for sourcing information on research ethics, and specific reference to Pasifika guidelines for research.

Introduction and rationale

Because ethical considerations must be addressed before starting on any observations as part of a research study, this chapter focuses particularly on the ethical aspects of observing for research purposes, and presents some frameworks for research ethics. As the authors of one such framework (Cullen *et al.* 2005: 1) point out, a framework can raise issues for many people involved in carrying out observations, such as:

- teachers as researchers;
- teachers invited to participate in colleagues' research;
- teachers invited to participate by outside researchers (for example, academic, postgraduate or contract researchers); and
- students and outsider researchers planning to approach centres to invite participation in observations.

Whether you plan to observe as part of a research project, or as part of pedagogical practice, reflecting on ethical issues is important.

Definitions and preliminary suggestions

Ethics is generally understood as people's endeavours to:

- live in appropriate, harmonious relationships with other people, with groups, or within institutions;

- take on moral responsibility for understanding the rightness or wrongness of their actions; and
- operate according to principles of fairness and justice.

(Grant and Riley 1991)

When preparing for observations, responsive, responsible relationships are important ethical considerations. This includes research by and for practitioners and teachers. As Zeni (2001: 164) notes, 'communication and collaboration are the best guides to preventing the ethical dilemmas of practitioner research'.

Before planning and carrying out observations in a responsible way, there are some basic suggestions to consider. It is important, for example, to:

- reflect on the process of being observed;
- negotiate access and permission to observe (this includes seeking in-formed consent from children, parents and teachers in an appropriate way that each person fully understands);
- prepare an explanation for participants that they have the right to with-draw (usually at any time until the observations are analysed);
- maintain privacy and prepare for confidentiality;
- include responsive feedback for participants;
- consider who owns the information collected; and
- use the information collected in appropriate ways (avoid harm or wrong, and seek to empower children, teachers, practitioners, families and com-munities).

Ethical frameworks

Various ethical frameworks are available to guide our reflections on how to observe appropriately and responsibly in educational settings. The British Ed-ucational Research Association has produced a code of practice for researchers set out in the *Revised Ethical Guidelines for Educational Research* (BERA 2011). For researchers across the social sciences, the Economic and Social Research Council has published a revised *Research Ethics Framework* (ESRC 2010) to guide the de-sign, implementation and oversight of research. These guidelines are focused on protecting those who participate in research projects and on promoting profes-sionalism in research. In Aotearoa New Zealand, the relevant updated guidelines are the Association for Research in Education Ethical Guidelines (New Zealand Association for Research in Education 2010).

Frameworks that focus specifically upon the ethical responsibilities of those who work with the youngest children include the *Code of Ethical Conduct and*

Statement of Commitment produced by the National Association for the Education of Young Children, in the USA (NAEYC 2005) and the *Code of Ethics* developed by Early Childhood Australia (2006). Both these documents set out aspirational values and principles for early childhood professionals to adhere to in their daily work. They provide a basis for ethical conduct and decision making that applies to observations undertaken as part of pedagogical practice and for research.

Two broad, overarching frameworks that are helpful when thinking through ethical issues relevant to observation for research purposes are David Flinders's (1992) framework developed in the United States, and a framework developed in New Zealand by Joy Cullen, Helen Hedges, and Jane Bone (2005, 2009) for early childhood research.

Flinders's framework

David Flinders (1992) has developed a useful approach for thinking about ethics throughout all phases of a research study. He describes four ethical bases for foreseeing ethical problems in qualitative research: *utilitarian, deontological, relational* and *ecological*. Utilitarian ethics tend to look at the positive and negative consequences of moral decisions. Deontological ethics emphasize conforming to ethical standards. Relational ethics focus on relationships in the field, and ecological ethics are concerned with respecting the environment and contexts in which the observations take place.

Flinders's approach has a parallel focus on the phases of research, and on foreseeing potential dilemmas at each phase of a study. The phases include recruitment, fieldwork and reporting. When we apply Flinders's perspectives to observing for research purposes, all four standpoints offer useful guidance and insights.

Utilitarian ethics highlight that, when planning research, it is important to seek parents' and teachers' informed consent and, where appropriate, children's assent before starting to observe (at the recruitment phase). It is then important to avoid harm when doing the observations (the fieldwork phase), and to maintain confidentiality when reporting the observations.

Similarly, McMillan and Meade (1985: 19) note that two conditions need to be met when undertaking observations:

- the permission of the person observed (or parent if necessary) has been obtained;
- the material recorded as a result of the observation is kept confidential.

They caution that, if you do not obtain permission and do not keep the findings of the observations confidential, the people under observation may understandably refuse to be observed by you (or anyone else) in the future.

The word 'deontological' simply refers to obligation. Deontological ethics focus on the obligation to embrace ethical standards such as honesty and justice. At the recruitment phase, reciprocity is important – meaning that the observations should be of mutual benefit and support. While collecting the observations, the emphasis is on avoidance of wrong, and fairness is a priority when reporting the observations.

Relational ethics move beyond a focus on rules and regulations to a regard for others. Flinders links relational ethics to feminist theories, including ideas about the ethics of caring. When inviting people to participate in observations, a collaborative approach is recommended. Throughout the observations, avoiding imposition is important, and when reporting observations and providing feedback, the experience should be confirming and affirming for the participants. The Code of Ethics published by Early Childhood Australia (2006) provides a good example of a relational approach to ethics because it articulates how early years professionals should act in relation to: children, families, colleagues, communities, students and employers, as well as to themselves and to research.

Ecological ethics, which are concerned with people's connections to the environment, focus on protection of human beings. When you are inviting participation in observations, cultural sensitivity is crucial. Throughout the process of observing, the observer avoids detachment, and responsive communication is essential when reporting the observations and discussing feedback with the participants.

Flinders (1992: 112) explains that relational ethics focus on 'respect for the people with whom we work and study', and states that

> ecological ethics strive to situate interdependent relationships within their broadest possible context. Here again, standards are redefined, but they are redefined with a particular emphasis on socially responsible modes of communication and the avoidance of detachment.

Cultural sensitivity

A key aspect of social responsibility in research is cultural awareness and sensitivity. This is crucial when planning, carrying out or writing observations. We all have a tendency to be egocentric, seeing things from our personal point of view, and ethnocentric, rooted in the values and understandings of our own social group. It is important to overcome these biases and to understand the values, expectations and life styles of children and families from different ethnic groups.

In New Zealand, for example, *Pasifika Education Research Guidelines* (prepared by Melani Anae and her colleagues, 2001) provide insightful guidance for using appropriate methodologies when planning observational research that is likely to involve children, adults or contexts connected to one or more of the Pasifika groups.[1] The authors stress the importance of: understanding and respecting cultural values; engaging in consultation processes; using suitable styles of communication; and considering participants' viewpoints at all stages of the research process. These strategies can be applied to observation and research with other minority groups.

Similarly, Carol Mutch's (2005) guide to participant research includes some helpful suggestions and cautions for non-Māori educational researchers/observers working with Māori people. It is important to consider who directs and owns research: Cram (2001: 49) suggests that 'research that is by Māori, for Māori will encourage Māori participation and Māori control over research processes'. Again, this insight can be applied more widely when considering how participation in observation processes may empower researchers and communities.

The main consideration when observing children, teachers, practitioners and family members in early childhood settings is *respect*. This emphasis is consistent with the principle of respectful relationships that overarches programming and practice in early childhood settings, and is embedded in *Te Whāriki* (Ministry of Education 1996) and in the Early Years Foundation Stage curriculum framework (DfES 2007).

Cullen, Hedges and Bone's framework for research ethics

In New Zealand, Cullen *et al.* (2005: 1) emphasize that their framework 'focuses on ethical dilemmas and issues specifically related to research in early childhood settings', and that 'it is also important to read and reflect on codes of ethics'. Such 'codes' would include sets of guidelines developed for research purposes and for professional practice mentioned above (e.g. BERA 2011; NAEYC 2005; Early Childhood Australia 2006).

As in Flinders's framework, phases of research mark out the different parts of Cullen *et al.*'s framework. The three phases, as applied to observation, are:

- planning the proposed observations;
- undertaking the observations; and
- disseminating the observations/research.

For each of the three parts or phases, there are three major areas with questions and matters for consideration: working with the under-fives; working in a team environment; and relationships with parents, families and communities. Some examples of questions for each phase, and how they might relate to observations, are set out in Table 5.1.

As Table 5.1 shows, when planning, doing and writing up observations it is important to be sensitive and responsive to infants, toddlers and young children, and to their families and communities. We need to be aware and alert to children's rights in observations. For example, at the planning stage, can the children assent to observations (that is, in addition to parental consent), and how will children benefit?

Priscilla Alderson (2004: 107), who has written extensively about children's perspectives in research, comments:

> When are children old enough to be competent to consent? There is no simple answer to this question. Much depends on each child's own experience and confidence, the type of research, and the skill with which researchers talk with children and help them to make unpressured, informed decisions. Children aged three years upwards have willingly taken part as researchers ...

The exemplar participant information and consent forms shown below (see Tables 5.2 and 5.3) are designed for adults and it takes imagination to design ways of communicating the equivalent information to young children. Observers can explain their planned observations to children using storyboards, drawings, photographs or diagrams, together with a simple script. Diagrams and signs (e.g. different facial expressions or thumbs up/thumbs down) can also be used for children to indicate assent.

Alderson also suggests that it is worthwhile asking children questions to gauge how much they understand about their rights and the process of the research (or observations). This can become a two-way process that helps us as researchers/observers to check out the clarity of our explanations and how well we are listening to children. It is also very worthwhile to check for continuing consent, to ensure that children continue to be comfortable with being observed.

There are further questions about processes and dissemination when working with 'under-fives', their parents, families and communities (see Table 5.1). One overarching consideration is that: 'Researchers need to consider ways that children can be empowered to participate in validation and dissemination processes' (Cullen *et al.* 2005: 5).

The use of photographs and video recordings can be a useful means of empowering children in this way but their use poses particular ethical challenges.

Table 5.1 Some questions about ethical issues when planning, doing and reporting observations

Research phase	Research environment		
	Working with the under-5s – observing infants, toddlers, children	**Working in a team environment**	**Relationships with parents, families and communities**
Planning the observations	Are the observations appropriate for the age group? Are the children able to assent? Who will benefit from the observations? How will non-consenting children be excluded (from written observation records, photographs, video or audio recordings)?	Which staff members need to agree to the observations taking place? Is voluntary participation of staff constrained by a power relationship? Are the observations likely to change team roles or group dynamics? Is the focus of the observations appropriate?	Do parents and caregivers understand fully the purpose of the observations and the processes for observing? Are there cultural beliefs that affect access or observation processes? Are informed consent procedures in place for each part of the observations (observing, taking notes, audio/video recording, photographs)? Have parents and families been informed about storage of data?
Doing the observations	Are there ongoing sensitivities or consent negotiations (e.g. does a child show discontent or ask you to stop observing)? Is the observer sensitive to the realities of the everyday teaching and learning process?	Are there sensitivities or ongoing consent negotiations? Is the right to withdraw from the observations until a particular point clear? Does the observer have a responsibility if she/he observes unacceptable practices?	Are there ongoing sensitivities or consent negotiations? Is the right to withdraw from the observations until a particular point clear?

Table 5.1 (*Continued*)

	Research environment		
Research phase	**Working with the under-5s – observing infants, toddlers, children**	**Working in a team environment**	**Relationships with parents, families and communities**
Writing up or reporting the observations (dissemination)	How will visual data collected for observations (photographs or video) be used in presenting assignments, talks or publications? Are there issues of anonymity and confidentiality? Can parents assist by discussing observations with children as a validation process? Is there a time limit on the use of visual data?	Can the teaching team use the observation for other purposes? Whose knowledge is valued in the assignment, presentation or publication? How will the observations be validated? What will happen if there are negative implications?	How will parents and families be informed about the observations/findings? Whose knowledge is valued in the assignment, presentation or publication? What will happen if there are negative implications? Have procedures for sharing the observations with parents/families been considered?

Source: Adapted for observation purposes from Cullen *et al.* (2005: 2–6).

Early years settings usually have clear policies concerning the collection, use and storage of images of children. Such policies and associated procedures are implemented for child protection and safeguarding and must be read and complied with carefully by observers/researchers. Visual data is not anonymous and people and places may be recognizable to potential viewers. There are, however, measures that can be put into place to protect confidentiality. For example, researchers can restrict access to images and store video data with coded labels that do not identify any participants by name.

Issues of consent to the taking and use of images are also complex. Discovering whether an adult or child is happy for their photograph to be taken, or is willing to be filmed, is relatively straightforward. It is important that their wishes are respected. Once the picture or film is taken, the participant(s) should then have the opportunity to view the image and decide whether they consent to its being kept and used. Papatheodorou *et al.* (2011) point out that it is important to explain to parents and children exactly how photographs and/or videos may subsequently be used, for example for study purposes only, for talks and conference presentations, or for possible publication (see also Table 5.1). Consent has to be gained for each type of use with clear agreement about the

Table 5.2 Example of an information sheet for a student observation project

[*Letterhead of higher education institution*]

[*Course name*]

Observation assignment: undertaking a running record

Students are to complete a 10-minute observation using the running record technique. The person observed may be an adult or a child.

Information for participants and/or parents

Thank you for agreeing to allow [*name of student*] to undertake this assignment. This task enables students to practise skills in using the 'running record' observational technique. This involves the student focusing upon an individual (adult or child) for a set period of time and noting down as much as possible of what that person says and does.

We have asked our students to carry out a 10-minute running record. The location and the timing of that running record may be negotiated between yourself and the student, but we suggest that a quieter time with few distractions will enable the student to record fuller details. You have the right to refuse to be involved in the observation, or to withdraw your permission at any point in the proceedings.

Your identity will be kept confidential – students are required to use only the initial of your first name/your child's first name, and to remove any identifying references (either locations or personal) from the observation.

The submitted observation task will be assessed on the basis of objectivity of language, depth and accuracy of descriptions, and whether confidentiality has been maintained. At no point would any comments be made by the observer about you (or your child) as an individual.

If you have any questions about this observational task, please do not hesitate to contact:

[*name of tutor*]

[*tutor role and name of course*]

[*contact telephone number and/or email address*]

Thank you for your assistance. Your support for our students' education course is appreciated.

Yours sincerely,

[*signature*] [*name*]
Course co-ordinator

period of time for which the images will be stored and used. Ownership of images should also be clarified as part of this consent process.

Ethics committees

Observations for research purposes are usually carried out only after approval from an ethics committee. This applies both to professional research and to research projects undertaken for undergraduate and postgraduate courses. Ethics committees check through detailed applications that explain how any planned research will comply with ethical protocols for the protection of researchers and research participants and the careful collection, storage, analysis and dissemination of data. Applicants must include copies of the proposed information sheets (and/or letters) and consent forms prepared for the participants in the observations. As a general example, an information sheet and consent form that were approved by one institution's ethics committee for a student teacher's observation assignment are given here (see Tables 5.2 and 5.3).

Table 5.3 Example of a consent form for a student observation project

---

[*Letterhead of higher education institution*]

I, _____
(parent/caregiver's name)

give

_____ (student's name)

permission to (please tick the appropriate box):

observe	Yes ☐	No ☐
use video recording	Yes ☐	No ☐
take photographs	Yes ☐	No ☐
use a tape recorder	Yes ☐	No ☐

of my child/children. I understand the above documentation forms part of the student's work that is marked by lecturers at

_____

[*higher education institution*].

Signed: _____

Date: _____

If photographs or video recordings contain any other child or children, permission must be obtained from the parent and/or caregiver of every child.

Summary

This chapter has raised ethical questions and dilemmas that can be considered before, during and after observing in education contexts and early childhood education settings for research purposes. A number of the ethical issues noted here concern the processes for recording observations, the use of visual data, validating and writing about observations. The next chapter continues to explore ways to record, validate, analyse and report on observations.

Note

1 'Pasifika' refers to peoples from the Island Nations in the South Pacific (Samoa, Tonga, Niue, the Cook Islands, Tokelau and Fiji).

6 Observational processes – how to record, analyse and report

This chapter is concerned mainly with observations carried out for research purposes. It includes some suggestions about how to prepare to observe, including reflections upon the role of the observer. It then focuses on recording and analysing observations, and addresses the reliability and validity of observations. There is an emphasis on the intentions, purpose and use of the observations. Examples from research studies are provided.

Preparation for observing

Before actually embarking on any observations for research purposes, the researcher must first reflect on the ethical issues. Formal approval or ethical clearance from an ethics committee (as discussed in Chapter 5) is almost always a requirement. After that, it is possible to invite participation, seeking the consent of all concerned and ensuring that participants understand what is involved.

Below are some practical suggestions about what to do when you are ready to observe (adapted from Gordon and Browne 1989, 2010):

- Enter and leave the area quietly. Keep in the background as much as possible.
- Sit in a low chair (or at ground level) in an out-of-the-way place. Sit where the activity of the children is unobstructed.
- Sit at the edge of an activity rather than right in the middle of it.
- Sometimes it may be necessary to follow children as they move from place to place. When that happens, be as inconspicuous as possible and be prepared for times when, for good reason, the teacher or child might object.
- Children may occasionally ask, 'What is your name? What are you doing? Why did you come here?' If asked a direct question, answer in a truthful, friendly manner, but be as brief as possible.

- Avoid a degree of response that will attract the children's attention, such as laughing at them, smiling, talking, or meeting their eyes.
- Avoid talking to other adults while observing.
- If a child is in obvious danger and no one else is around, the observer should step in. Call for a teacher only if there is time.

Several of the above suggestions have their origins in the child-study movement (discussed in Chapter 1). Sociocultural approaches to planning and carrying out observations view children and adults more as active participants in observations and observational assessments (as highlighted in Chapter 3). However, a key principle across all observational processes and approaches is to relate to infants, children and adults with respect. It is also essential that children's care and learning are not disrupted by a researcher's presence or activities.

The role of the observer

When preparing to observe it is important to consider the type of observer role to adopt and the impact that such decisions may have upon the observations. Qualitative methods may demand a participatory role (a high level of involvement in the activities of the early years setting) while quantitative observation techniques usually require a non-participant stance. In addition, a researcher may be an 'insider' in a setting, for example observing in one's own workplace, or an 'outsider' entering an unfamiliar context. Papatheodorou *et al.* (2011) explore how these observer roles (participant/non-participant and insider/ outsider) may intersect and influence the research. For example, non-participant observers who are outsiders will be able to adopt an objective viewpoint but they may not fully understand the context for their research.

Even when the observer's aim is to be neutral and maintain objectivity, the act of observing will be influenced by her or his prior experiences and emotional state. Caring for babies and young children and sharing in their experiences often engenders strong feelings. The emotions that observing evokes can sometimes be used to add insight to a study. In Elfer's (2005) work with a group of master's degree students, who were also early years professionals, the feelings aroused when closely observing children led them to question how care was given and received. Hanne Warming conducted participant observations with children in a day nursery, taking a 'least adult role', 'listening with all the senses' (Warming 2005: 55) and becoming fully socially and emotionally involved. This provided opportunities for her to share in children's day-to-day experiences and to appreciate and reflect upon their points of view.

Recording observations

When planning observations it is also necessary to make decisions about how to record them and what equipment will be needed. As outlined in Table 5.1, before the researcher starts to observe and record, consent is needed for all parts of the observation, including (where appropriate):

- observing;
- recording notes in writing;
- audio recording;
- video recording; and
- taking photographs.

Written notes, observational schedules, rating scales and templates

Back in 1949, Marie Bell systematically recorded her observations of children and adults by writing in a notebook that she carried in her pocket (see Chapter 1). Observations are still often recorded, simply and effectively, by writing detailed notes in a notebook or exercise book.

Event recordings, category recordings and rating scales are usually coded on sheets prepared in advance (as explained and presented in Chapter 3; an observation sheet for running records is also given in Table 3.14). These sheets or templates may be attached to a clipboard and carried by the observer. A timing device is often needed. This may be a stopwatch or electronic beeper to mark the time intervals for observing and recording.

Audio recordings

Audio recordings, which provide a more complete record of speech and verbal interactions, may be used to supplement written notes. Small lapel microphones with radio transmitters are sometimes attached to individual children to provide clearer records of their speech. The recording is picked up by a nearby receiver. This can be effective for accuracy, but is also rather intrusive – children need to assent to this technique, and need time to become familiar with the equipment.

It is also possible for the observer to speak into a microphone or dictaphone to record details. However, we would not generally recommend this practice, as it may be intrusive and exacerbate the noise levels in the children's environment.

Video recordings

Video provides a useful means of collecting and storing visible and audible data (McDonald 1986). Video recordings can be replayed repeatedly to classify and analyse observational data using multiple techniques, both qualitative and quantitative. When making videos to record observations, it is important to make sure that the faces of key participants are clearly visible. It is also essential to exclude or erase non-consenting persons from the recording or picture.

Photographs

Photographic images are useful for recording the setting and the environment, making it easier to understand the observations in context. They can illustrate children's strengths and interests, their dispositions, and changes over time. The same consent requirements apply as for video recordings.

Ethnography

Ethnographic studies usually use multiple research methods, and may use a range of recording techniques. In her ethnographic study of children in the outdoors, Alison Stephenson (1999) used a variety of recording techniques, which she introduced sensitively over time. Over a two-month period she made 38 fieldwork visits to the early childhood centre she was studying. At first she made detailed field notes, and when she felt children were comfortable about this, she started using a camera, a tape recorder, and later a video camera to record her observations.

Learning Stories and ICT

Learning Stories may be recorded directly onto a prepared template (see Table 6.1). This can be done by hand but laptop computers, digital cameras or video recorders are also frequently used. The documentation of Learning Stories has involved an increasingly wide range of ICT. The template presented in Table 6.1 was developed by the Education Leadership Project, managed by Wendy Lee and funded by the New Zealand Ministry of Education. Learning Stories have been documented in many forms, including handwritten narratives, computer-generated narratives, film-based and digital photographs, video footage, and examples of children's work.

Table 6.1 Learning Stories: template from the Educational Leadership Project

Child's name:
Teacher: Date:

		Examples or cues	A Learning Story
Belonging	**Taking an interest**	Finding an interest here – a topic, an activity, a role Recognizing the familiar, enjoying the unfamiliar Coping with change	
Well-being	**Being involved**	Paying attention for a sustained period, feeling safe, trusting others Being playful with others and/or materials	
Exploration	**Persisting with difficulty**	Setting and choosing difficult tasks Using a range of strategies to solve problems when 'stuck' (be specific)	
Communication	**Expressing an idea or feeling**	In a range of ways (specify) For example: oral language, gesture, music, art, writing, using numbers and patterns, telling stories	
Contribution	**Taking responsibility**	Responding to others, to stories, and imagined events, ensuring that things are fair, self-evaluating, helping others, contributing to programme	

What learning is going on here?

Question: What learning did I think went on here (i.e. the main points of the Learning Story?)

Pathways and possibilities

Questions: How might we encourage this interest, ability, strategy, disposition, story to
• be more complex;
• appear in different activities in the programme?
How might we encourage the next 'step' in the Learning Story framework?

Source: Wendy Lee, personal communication, February 2006.

As is explained in the *Kei Tua o te Pae* resource 'Information and communication technology (ICT)' (Ministry of Education 2009), the range of equipment (or tools) used to record Learning Stories can include cameras (both still and digital), audio and video recorders, computers, scanners and photocopiers. Children's contributions to Learning Stories provide exciting opportunities for them to use their developing skills in the use of ICT to express their points of view. In her research in a UK context, Rebecca Webster (2010) provided children with hand-held digital cameras to enable them to tell their own stories, about home and school, and establish their identities as learners and researchers.

Analysing and reporting observations

A first step in analysing observations is to ensure that they are meaningful, accurate and consistent. Bruce McMillan and Anne Meade (1985: 16) pointed out very clearly that:

> The most important consideration when undertaking observational studies is making sure that what is being observed is important, and likely to be of value to the teacher, parent or whoever is undertaking the study . . . Where observational records are to be used for specific purposes, every attempt should be made to reach a level of accuracy and reliability.

Quantitative approaches

When using quantitative approaches to analyse observations, the reliability and appropriateness of the observations are key concerns:

> Quantitative designs provide rigorous methods of investigating children's behaviour but to be of high quality the measures used must be reliable and valid. *Reliability* refers to the consistency and repeatability of the measure used whilst *validity* concerns the appropriateness and meaningfulness of inferences . . .
>
> (Aubrey *et al.* 2000: 56)

Observations using precoded categories (as shown in the example of a completed precoded form from Podmore and Craig 1991, in Chapter 3) are more likely to be reliable and valid if the categories are meaningful, clearly defined and comprehensive. The behavioural categories also need to be relevant to the participants, and to the purposes and planned use of the observations. Consistency between observers and stability across time are both important.

Interobserver reliability

Reliability is particularly important when observations are analysed quantitatively. Observations should be replicable – repeatable – and consistent, not only between observers, but also over time.

Interobserver reliability shows the extent to which observations are consistent across two or more observers when they are observing the same people and environments at the same time, or rating precisely the same excerpts of an audio or video recording. When observing and coding over several days, weeks or months, it is important to do interobserver reliability checks quite regularly. This is useful as a check for 'observer drift' – a situation in which observers may interpret and code differently as time moves on.

Agreement between observers may be checked by calculating the percentage in this way:

$$\text{Percentage} = \frac{\text{number of agreements}}{\text{number of agreements} + \text{number of disagreements}} \times \frac{100}{1}$$

Ideally, interobserver agreement should be around 85 per cent or more, but agreement of over 70 per cent is generally acceptable. This type of percentage calculation is likely to be sufficiently accurate and robust only if the observers are simultaneously coding exactly the same time segment of behaviour. This means that observers need to be able to account for agreements, disagreements and omissions each time they code a category.

For example, in a study of infants in childcare centres, the observers collected interobserver reliability data on 20 per cent of the total observations (Podmore and Craig 1991). Reliability checks were spread across the months during which the observations took place. The calculations of reliability were strict, because we were able to check, across both observers' coding forms, each instance of a behaviour recorded during each 15-second time slot. Across three observers, the reliability percentages for each category ranged from 75 to 100, with a satisfactory mean of 87.78 per cent (see Table 6.2).

As explained above, it is important to check that each observer is observing and recording the same behaviour at the same time, and that no coding is missed or omitted.

Table 6.2 Interobserver reliability percentages across caregiver–infant behaviour categories

Observational category	Reliability* (%)
Caregiver talk	89.89
Caregiver play	81.48
Caregiver mediates objects	80.77
Caregiver touches/hugs/holds	83.33
Caregiver expresses positive affect	90.00
Caregiver expresses negative affect	100.00
Caregiver restricts, forbids, intrudes	85.71
Caregiver's positive response to social bid	81.82
Caregiver ignores request, negative response	100.00
Infant talks/babbles to caregiver	82.46
Infant touches/hugs caregiver	84.00
Shares object with caregiver	83.33
Express positive affect to caregiver	90.00
Express negative affect to caregiver	75.00
Asks caregiver for object	100.00
Violates adult standards	100.00
Interacts with peers	86.41
Solitary activity	91.50
Mean percentage across all categories	88.09

*Mean percentage of agreement between observers
Source: Podmore and Craig (1991: 54).

Statistical analyses and reporting

The next step in quantitative analysis is usually to describe the number of instances on which each behaviour is observed, and/or their duration. These descriptive statistics are often presented in the form of tables or graphs. Helpful introductory information on analysing and presenting quantitative data is presented in Penny Mukherji and Deborah Albon's (2010) book on research methods. The *Researching Effective Pedagogy in the Early Years* report (Siraj-Blatchford *et al.* 2002) provides examples of graphical presentation of descriptive data. It shows the proportions of different types of pedagogical interactions occurring in various contexts, based upon analysis of close observations undertaken in case study settings.

Quantitative reports of observational studies usually emphasize objectivity and reliability. They almost always include tables of numerical data and accurate presentation of statistical analyses. The writing is precise and concise. On the whole, quantitative reports are written in the third person, so that the writer refers to her or himself as 'the observer' or 'the researcher(s)'. However, in some more recent studies this detached, impersonal style of writing is changing.

Qualitative approaches

It is desirable for qualitative research approaches to be meaningful, appropriate and robust.

Validation

Validity is important in qualitative approaches. Validity checks ensure that observations accurately depict what they are designed to show, and that observations are meaningful and 'ring true' to practitioners. Observational data may be validated by individual people or by groups.

One example of a group validation process is provided by the *A'oga Fa'a Samoa*, the first Pasifika centre to be selected as a New Zealand early childhood centre of innovation (COI). As part of a three-year action research project, educators ('teacher-researchers') at the centre carried out observations, with support from a research associate. 'Respondent validation' was facilitated through a focus/advisory group. This group, which included teachers, parents, management, and the research associates who worked alongside the teachers, took a key role in validation. Group members commented on and contributed to the action research processes, the observations, the translations of the narrative observations from Samoan to English and the findings from the centre (Podmore *et al.* 2005).

Triangulation is widely accepted by researchers as a useful process for enhancing validity (Aubrey *et al.* 2000; McMurray *et al.* 2004). Triangulation can mean:

- using multiple ways to collect data; or
- using several theories to interpret data; or
- drawing on multiple participant perspectives (across several researchers, observers or participant groups) to see if different data or perspectives corroborate each other.

The trustworthiness of qualitative observations

While some researchers apply the scientific standards of objectivity, reliability and validity to qualitative research (as explained above), others argue that qualitative research is based upon different philosophical values and so alternative criteria should be applied when judging qualitative research. Lincoln and Guba (1985) were pioneers in developing and describing methods for ensuring the quality of naturalistic enquiry. They propose the following principles:

- confirmability (objectivity);
- dependability (reliability);
- credibility (internal validity); and
- transferability (external validity).

Dependability and confirmability can be claimed when written accounts of observations or research are coherent and plausible to the reader, corresponding with their own knowledge and expectations. Credibility and transferability are achieved through readers recognizing and believing the research and linking what is reported to their own experience.

Laurel Richardson (1998) proposes 'crystallization' as an alternative to triangulation. She argues that triangles are rigid and two-dimensional whereas crystals combine 'symmetry and substance with an infinite variety of shapes, substances, transmutations, multidimenionalities and angles of approach' (p. 358). The metaphor of crystallization is a useful one for qualitative researchers. Like 'triangulation' it emphasizes the importance of structure and consistency to enhance validity. It also allows for a research topic to be viewed from different facets, allowing for the possibility of multiple perspectives that may not corroborate directly.

Such multiple perspectives are included in observations that contribute to the pedagogical documentation that forms a key part of the learning and research in Reggio Emilia pre-schools (see Chapter 3). Here it is acknowledged that observations are not objective or neutral and so there is a need for 'rigorous subjectivity' through which biases and interpretations are made explicit and discussed (Rinaldi 2006).

Qualitative analyses and reporting

Traditionally, the child-study movement was associated with detailed written observations of individual children, usually recorded in the form of running records. On the basis of repeated observations of an individual child, made on three to five occasions on different observational days, observers (or student teachers) would note a child's behaviour, focusing on each of the developmental domains (physical, cognitive, language and socio-emotional). They sometimes highlighted examples of each domain of development on the running record transcripts.

Observations carried out as part of ethnographic studies (and also Learning Stories) are not fragmented into domains of development. In New Zealand, the introduction of *Te Whāriki* (Ministry of Education 1996) brought new ways of assessing children's learning (described in Chapter 3). When the emphasis moved to sociocultural approaches and the use of Learning Stories (Carr 2001; Cowie and Carr 2009) the analyses and reporting became more holistic.

Many qualitative research studies search for, identify and discuss key themes emerging across the observations or other data. In the ethnographic studies that led on to the development of Teaching Stories using the Child's Questions (see Chapter 4) detailed narratives were recorded directly on to laptop computers (Podmore and May 1998). The observational focus was on children, adults and contexts, and in relation to the principles and strands of *Te Whāriki*. The principles of *Te Whāriki* provided an overarching holistic framework, and we sorted the observations using NUD*IST, a computer program that helped to organize the large amount of observational data from seven different early childhood centres. NVIVO is a similar computer program, now commonly used to help sort and categorize key themes in qualitative studies.

In Australia, Fleer and Richardson's (2004, 2009) approach used Rogoff's three lenses for observing and analysing. As explained in Chapter 3, these areas of focus when making observations or analysing them are the personal, the interpersonal and the cultural. Using this approach, teachers can analyse a narrative observation of a small group of children and adult/s in various ways – for example, by:

- looking at social influences;
- considering the influence of culture on the individual child;
- focusing on the transformation of participation for one individual child;
- emphasizing the interactions between the adult/teacher and a child/children (interpersonal focus); and
- focusing on the cultural or institutional aspects, like the centre's philosophy, to make sense of the observations and make their interpretation meaningful.

(Fleer and Richardson 2009: 134–6)

Whether observations and assessments are carried out as part of teaching practice or as part of research studies, ideally there is an emphasis on reporting the observations in a way that is holistic, empowering and meaningful. Reports written about qualitative studies are most often written in the first person (the observer/the researcher becomes 'I' or 'we'). Validity is important and the tone when writing about the observations is reflective.

The impact of observational research upon practice

Care and attention to detail in the processes of recording, analysing and re-porting are particularly important in educational research, where findings may influence practice. In the UK, several practitioner-led research projects were funded by the Children's Workforce Development Council between 2006 and 2010. These included a number of projects involving observation in early child-hood settings (CWDC 2011).

Once observational research is shared and published it may have a wider impact upon policy and provision and/or the ways in which educators work and respond to children. There are several examples throughout this book of the part that observation-based research has played in the development of early childhood education. In New Zealand, the UK and elsewhere, both large-scale and small-scale projects have been, and will continue to be, influential for the development of curriculum and pedagogy.

Summary

When recording and analysing observations, it is always important to consider carefully who owns the written, audio and visual observations (data), how the observational records are stored, and what happens to the observational data. These considerations are important throughout all phases of planning, carrying out, writing up and reporting observations.

Conclusion: Observing for research and practice – some key voices

The main purpose of this chapter is to summarize the usefulness and delights of observing. The chapter includes voices from several experienced observers. There are some clear links to teaching practice and to observational research processes.

The usefulness and delights of observing

Several writers strongly endorse the usefulness of sociocultural observations for and by teachers. Marilyn Fleer and Carmel Richardson (2009) express enthusiasm about the relevance of sociocultural approaches to teachers' everyday observations and their assessments of children's learning:

> In taking a sociocultural approach to assessment, early childhood educators will be able to record broader, richer and culturally embedded data on the groups of children they interact with each day in their centres. This will allow for more meaningful assessments to be made about learning and teaching. Teachers will find the 'teachable moments' (Fleer, 2003) when the majority of observations should take place.
>
> (Fleer and Richardson 2009:143–4)

They see the theoretical knowledge that supports sociocultural observations as meaningful and well worth acquiring. From her perspective as an early childhood teacher, Carmel Richardson concludes that:

> Adopting a sociocultural approach to observing and planning has challenged me to rethink my understanding of how children learn and develop. The new approach demands a greater focus on how children interact with each other and adults to co-construct knowledge and understanding. It is not always easy or obvious to record this dynamic process. The cultural–institutional lens has challenged me to question the 'norms' I have always adopted and encouraged me to analyse my

observations in different cultural ways ... I now notice what I am privileging and what I am silencing ... Sociocultural observations, with their focus on interactions, scaffolded learning and cultural interpretations, provide strong evidence to support the notion that every child is rich, powerful and competent.

(Fleer and Richardson 2004: 46)

As Fleer and Richardson point out, sociocultural approaches to learning and assessment are useful, challenging and exciting for early childhood teachers. Potentially, they empower children to learn appropriately within culturally diverse settings.

Observations are integral to assessment. The Learning Stories approach to observation and assessment is associated with reflective teaching and learning, and encourages collaborative enquiry and discussion among teachers. In learning and applying this approach, educators must engage with the complexity of assessment. Bronwen Cowie and Margaret Carr (2009) believe that considering new assessment formats can help to:

- establish a social community of early childhood educators who want to discuss learning and assessment;
- provide spaces for new ideas about assessment and its relationship with learning;
- invite educators to think about their own learning and try out new ideas.

It is clearly important to connect observations, assessments, policies and practices in ways that are meaningful for children and adults. Mary Fawcett (2009: 21) contends:

Observation is a vital research tool but also – especially when embedded in reflective dialogue with others – an endless source of information and constant stimulus to discovering how people of all ages think and relate to each other.

Two personal accounts

The two examples of 'key voices' that are included in this section provide personal accounts about observing. First, Lesley Rameka shares some of her experiences of the delights and purpose of observations and assessments with young children. The example in Table 7.1 is about observing as part of pedagogical practice:

Table 7.1 Some comments on observation and assessment

The challenge for educators, I believe, is to capture the warmth, humour, and joy of children's learning. This requires that we do not stand back as cold, aloof, unbiased observers, but embroil ourselves enthusiastically in the process, celebrating the learning.

I think meaningful observations and assessment are about seeing rather than looking. It's akin to putting on a pair of glasses that allows you to see what was previously not noticed. What is so exciting about this is that once you put the glasses on they don't come off and a whole new world of understandings and learnings opens up for you.

One of the key questions for me about observations and assessment is: Who are the observations being written for? I believe observations should be written for me, 'nanny'. They should be meaningful for me in that they must reflect positively and warmly my *mokopuna* [grandchild], celebrating her successes, achievements and strengths. They should be able to be understood by me, written in language that I can understand, and in this way they should invite my interest and involvement in the assessment process.

Lesley Rameka, February 2006

Next, Sarah Te One reflects on her experiences of observing children in early childhood centres as part of her PhD research. She gives thoughtful comments about the process of doing observational research (see Table 7.2).

Concluding comments

When starting observations, as we have seen, some important points concern:

- the need to give full consideration to ethics before starting observing, and at all stages during the observation;
- being careful about making judgements; and
- discerning how to embrace a credit-based approach.

As highlighted in this chapter, an important priority is to be holistic and empower children, parents, educators and their communities.

In practice this means that, although a wide variety of approaches to observational research and practice is available (as discussed in Chapters 3 and 4), there is strong support for the notion of observing holistically – that is, in a way that acknowledges children's holistic learning, development and life experiences. This is consistent with the principle of holistic development in *Te Whāriki* (the New Zealand early childhood curriculum), which states that 'the early childhood curriculum reflects the holistic way children learn and grow' (Ministry of Education 1996: 41). It also means that observation is ideally an empowering process (as explained in relation to ethics in Chapter 5) that respects children, the environment, and teachers, parents and communities.

Table 7.2 Reflections on my current research processes

Having time to sit and watch children and adults go about their day-to-day play and work in a centre was a luxury. I remember the first day of observations – the clean notebook, the new document on the laptop and a sense of freedom, I suppose. I could observe what and how I wanted (within the bounds of the ethics agreement, of course). In a sense, it was overwhelming – where do I start? In the end, it began with who was in front of me, and I wrote and wrote and wrote some more.

While they say first impressions count, I found that during the observation phase I had to revisit what I had noted. The longer you are in a place, the more you understand why and how things happen the way they do. The reflective thinking about what I had seen and heard meant that I added both breadth and depth to the context of the observations. What seemed on the surface to be a very simple task – write down what you see and hear – I found myself immersed in asking more and more questions about why I saw and heard what I did – what other influences were there? And in that way, I found my field notes, which were initially running records, became a springboard for more ideas about what to look for. I would make a point of watching one thing for an hour, or being in a different place to watch things, or, as I became a familiar figure in the centres, interacting with children as part of observing, too.

I loved observing children in my study centres, but I totally underestimated how exhausting it could be. After a day of writing down observations during the fieldwork stage of my data collection, I would arrive home, my head buzzing with impressions. Rather than the question of what to observe, at times it became a question of what not to observe. Everything seemed relevant en route to gaining a holistic understanding of the context. I realised, too, that this was not going to be possible in a month – you can start with observing the obvious activity in front of you, but the layers of complex interactions between people, places and things would take forever. The combination of photos, interviews, centre documents and the observations helped to reveal, partially at least, the complex mechanics of how centres function.

Sarah Te One, February 2006

There are certainly delights associated with observing. Anne Smith (1998: 41) describes observation as 'a fascinating activity and a useful tool' and Cathy Nutbrown (2006: 129) enthuses: 'Children's learning is so complex, so rich, so fascinating, so varied and so full of enthusiasm that to see it take place every day, before one's very eyes, is one of the greatest privileges of any early childhood practitioner.' We agree with them. Observing children, adults and their environments can be an extremely interesting, joyful and worthwhile experience. Systematic observations contribute to knowledge about young children's worlds, and about learning and development in context. They can help teachers to provide high-quality education and contribute to communication with and among families.

References

Albon, D. (2007) Food for thought: the importance of food and eating in early childhood practice, in J. R. Moyles (ed.) *Early Years Foundations: Meeting the Challenge*. Maidenhead: McGraw-Hill/Open University Press.

Alcock, S. J. (2005) A sociocultural interpretation of young children's playful and humorous communication. Unpublished PhD thesis, Massey University, Palmerston North.

Alderson, P. (2004) Ethics, in S. Fraser, V. Lewis, S. Ding, M. Kellett and C. Robinson (eds) *Doing Research with Children and Young People*. London: Sage Publications.

Anae, M., Coxon, E., Mara, D., Wendt-Samu, T. and Finau, C. (2001) *Pasifika Education Research Guidelines*. Report to the Ministry of Education, Research Division. Auckland: Auckland Uniservices Ltd. http://www.educationcounts .govt.nz/_data/assets/pdf_file/0010/7669/pacrsrch–guide.pdf [Accessed 30 July 2011].

Anning, A., Cullen, J. and Fleer, M. (2009) *Early Childhood Education: Society and Culture*, 2nd edition. London: Sage Publications.

Arnold, C. (1999) *Child Development and Learning Two to Five Years: Georgia's Story*. Abingdon: Hodder and Stoughton.

Arnold, C. (2003) *Observing Harry: Child Development and Learning 0–5*. Maidenhead: Open University Press.

Athey, C. (1991) *Extending Thought in Young Children*. London: Paul Chapman Publishing.

Aubrey, C., David, T., Godfrey, R. and Thompson, L. (2000) *Early Childhood Educational Research: Issues in Methodology and Ethics*. London: RoutledgeFalmer.

Bancroft, S., Fawcett, M. and Hay, P. (2008) *Researching Children Researching the World: 5 × 5 × 5 = Creativity*. Stoke on Trent: Trentham.

Bandura, A. (1977) *Social Learning Theory*. Englewood Cliffs, NJ: Prentice Hall.

Bandura, A. (1997) Self-efficacy, *The Harvard Mental Health Letter*, March: 4–6.

Beeby, C. E. (1992) *The Biography of an Idea: Beeby on Education* (Educational Research Series No. 69). Wellington: New Zealand Council for Educational Research.

BERA (British Educational Research Association) (2011) *Ethical Guidelines for Educational Research*. London: British Educational Research Association.

http://www.bera.ac.uk/files/2011/08/BERA-Ethical-Guidelines-2011.pdf [Accessed 30 November 2011].

Bick, E. (1964) Notes on infant observation in psychoanalytic training, *International Journal of Psychoanalysis*, 45: 558–66.

Bluma, S., Shearer, M.S., Frohman, A. and Hilliard, J. (1976) *Portage Guide to Early Education: Checklist*. Portage, WI: Portage Project.

Brennan, M. (2005) 'They just want to be with us.' Young children learning to live the culture. A post-Vygotskian analysis of young children's enculturation into a childcare setting. Unpublished PhD thesis, Victoria University of Wellington, Wellington.

Briggs, A. (2002) *Surviving Space: Papers on Infant Observation*. London: Karnac.

Bronfenbrenner, U. (1979) *The Ecology of Human Development*. Cambridge, MA: Harvard University Press.

Bronfenbrenner, U. (1986) Ecology of the family as a context for human development: research perspectives, *Developmental Psychology*, 22(6): 723–42.

Bronfenbrenner, U. (2004) *Making Human Beings Human: Bioecological Perspectives on Human Development*. Thousand Oaks, CA: Sage Publications.

Bruner, J. (1990) *Acts of Meaning*. Cambridge, MA: Harvard University Press.

Bruner, J. (1996) *The Culture of Education*. Cambridge, MA: Harvard University Press.

Cardno, C.E.M. (2003) *Action Research: A Developmental Approach*. Wellington: NZCER Press.

Carr, M. (2001) *Assessment in Early Childhood Settings: Learning Stories*. London: Sage Publications.

Carr, M., May, H. and Podmore, V. N. (with Cubey, P., Hatherly, A. and Macartney, B.) (2000) *Learning and Teaching Stories: Action Research on Evaluation in Early Childhood*. Wellington: New Zealand Council for Educational Research and Ministry of Education.

Claxton, G. and Carr, M. (2004) A framework for teaching learning: the dynamics of disposition, *Early Years*, 24(1): 87–97.

Coates, D. and Thomson, W. (2010) Using Learning Stories in the Early Years Foundation Stage, in I. Palaiologou (ed.) *The Early Years Foundation Stage: Theory and Practice*. London: Sage Publications.

Collins, S., Gibbs, J., Luff, P., Thomas, L. and Sprawling, M. (2010) Thinking through the uses of observation and documentation, in J. Moyles (ed.) *Thinking About Play: Developing a Reflective Approach*. Maidenhead: McGraw-Hill/Open University Press.

Cowie, B. and Carr, M. (2009) The consequences of sociocultural assessment, in A. Anning, J. Cullen and M. Fleer (eds) *Early Childhood Education: Society and Culture*, 2nd edition. London: Sage Publications.

Cram, F. (2001) Rangahau Māori: Tona Tika, Tona Poro/the validity and integrity of Māori research, in M. Tolich (ed.) *Research Ethics in Aotearoa New Zealand*. Auckland: Pearson Education.

Cullen, J. (2001) An introduction to understanding learning, in V. Carpenter, H. Dixon, E. Rata and C. Rawlinson (eds) *Theory in Practice for Educators*. Palmerston North: Dunmore Press.

Cullen, J., Hedges, H. and Bone, J. (2005) *Planning, Undertaking and Disseminating Research in Early Childhood Settings: An Ethical Framework*. http://www.childforum.com/research/on-doing-new-research-ethics-publishing/70-ethical-guide-for-researching-in-early-childhood-settings.html [Accessed 30 July 2011].

Cullen, J., Hedges, H. and Bone, J. (2009) Planning, undertaking and disseminating research in early childhood settings: an ethical framework, *New Zealand Research in Early Childhood Education*, 12: 109–18.

Cunningham, P. (2006) Early years teachers and the influence of Piaget: evidence from oral history, *Early Years*, 26(1): 5–16.

CWDC (Children's Workforce Development Council) (2011) *Practitioner-Led Research (PLR)*. http://www.cwdcouncil.org.uk/plr [Accessed 30 July 2011].

Dahlberg, G., Moss, P. and Pence, A. (1999) *Beyond Quality in Early Childhood Education: Postmodern Perspectives*. London: Falmer Press.

Darwin, C. R. (1877) A biographical sketch of an infant, *Mind. A Quarterly Review of Psychology and Philosophy*, 2(7) (July): 285–94. http://darwin-online.org.uk/pdf/1877_infant_F1779.pdf [Accessed 30 July 2011].

DCELLS (Department for Children, Education, Lifelong Learning and Skills) (2008) *Observing Children*. Cardiff: Welsh Assembly Government.

DCSF (Department for Children, Schools and Families) (2008) *Statutory Framework for the Early Years Foundation Stage*. Nottingham: DCSF Publications.

DENI (Department of Education, Northern Ireland) 2006 *Curricular Guidance for Pre-School Education*. Belfast: Northern Ireland Council for the Curriculum, Examinations and Assessment. http://www.deni.gov.uk/preschoolguidance.pdf [Accessed 30 July 2011].

DES (Department of Education and Science) (1990) *Starting with Quality: The Report of the Committee of Enquiry into the Quality of Experience offered to 3 to 4-year-olds*. London: HMSO.

Densem, A. and Chapman, B. (2000) *Learning Together: The Playcentre Way*. Auckland: New Zealand Playcentre Federation.

DfES (Department for Education and Skills) (2002) *Birth to Three Matters*. London: DfES Publications.

DfES (2004a) *Choice for Parents, the Best Start for Children: A Ten Year Childcare Strategy*. London: DfES Publications.

DfES (2004b) *Every Child Matters: Change for Children.* London: DfES Publications.

DfES (2007) *The Early Years Foundation Stage.* Nottingham: DfES Publications.

Drummond, M. J. (1993) *Assessing Children's Learning.* London: David Fulton.

Early Childhood Australia (2006) *Code of Ethics.* http://www.early childhoodaustralia.org.au/pdf/code_of_ethics/code_of_ethics_%20 brochure_screenweb_2010.pdf [Accessed 30 July 2011].

Elfer, P. (2005) Observation matters, in L. Abbott and A. Langston (eds) *Birth to Three Matters.* Maidenhead: Open University Press.

Elfer, P. (2007) Babies and young children in nurseries: using psychoanalytic ideas to explore tasks and interactions, *Children and Society,* 21(2): 111–22.

Elfer, P. and Dearnley, K. (2007) Nurseries and emotional well-being: evaluating an emotionally containing model of professional development, *Early Years,* 27(3): 267–79.

ESRC (Economic and Social Research Council) (2010) *Research Ethics Framework.* http://www.esrc.ac.uk/_images/Framework_for_Research_Ethics_tcm8-4586.pdf [Accessed 30 July 2011].

Fawcett, M. (2009) *Learning Through Child Observation,* 2nd edition. London: Jessica Kingsley Publishers.

Flanders, N. A. (1960) *Interaction Analysis in the Classroom.* Minneapolis, MN: University of Michigan.

Fleer, M. (2002) Sociocultural assessment in early years education: myth or reality?, *International Journal of Early Years Education,* 10(2): 105–20.

Fleer, M. B. and Richardson, C. (2004) *Observing and Planning in Early Childhood Settings: Using a Sociocultural Approach.* Watson, ACT: Early Childhood Australia.

Fleer, M. B. and Richardson, C. (2009) Mapping the transformation of understanding, in A. Anning, J. Cullen and M. Fleer (eds) *Early Childhood Education: Society and Culture,* 2nd edition. London: Sage Publications.

Fleer, M., Anning, A. and Cullen, J. (2009) A framework for conceptualizing early childhood education, in A. Anning, J. Cullen and M. Fleer (eds) *Early Childhood Education: Society and Culture,* 2nd edition. London: Sage Publications.

Flinders, D. (1992) In search of ethical guidance: constructing a basis for dialogue, *Qualitative Studies in Education,* 3(2): 101–13.

Forman, G. and Hall, E. (2005) Wondering with children: the importance of observation in early education, *Early Childhood Research and Practice,* 7(2). http://ecrp.uiuc.edu/v7n2/forman.html [Accessed 19 October 2011].

Foster, P. (1996) *Observing Schools: A Methodological Guide.* London: Paul Chapman.

Freud, S. ([1940]2001) *An Outline of Psychoanalysis. The Standard Edition of the Complete Psychological Works of Sigmund Freud, Volume 23* (Translated by J. Strachey in collaboration with A. Freud). London: Vintage.

Galton, M., Simon, B. and Croll, P. (1980) *Inside the Primary Classroom*. London: Routledge and Kegan Paul.

Galton, M., Hargreaves, L., Comber, C., Pell, T. and Wall, D. (1999) *Inside the Primary Classroom: 20 Years On*. London: Routledge.

Gesell, A. (1950) A pictorial survery of preschool behaviour, Chapter 5 in *The First Five Years of Life*. London: Methuen and Co. Ltd.

Gordon, A. M. and Browne, K. W. (1989) *Beginnings and Beyond: Foundations in Early Childhood Education*. Clifton Park, NY: Delmar Learning.

Gordon, A. M. and Browne, K. W. (2010) *Beginnings and Beyond: Foundations in Early Childhood Education*, 8th edition. Clifton Park, NY: Delmar Learning.

Grant, W. and Riley, D. (1991) Ethics and educators: today. Paper presented at the annual conference of the Australian Association for Research in Education, Surfers Paradise, Queensland.

Grey, A. L. (1975) *Look and Listen*. Auckland: New Zealand Playcentre Federation.

Hamer, C. (1999) *Observation: A Tool for Learning. Te tirohanga, he taonga* āwhina *i te ako*. Wellington: The Open Polytechnic of New Zealand.

Harms, T. and Clifford, R. M. (1980) *Early Childhood Environment Rating Scale*. New York: Teachers College Press.

Harms, T. and Clifford, R. M. (1989) *Family Day Care Rating Scale*. New York: Teachers College Press.

Harms, T., Cryer, D. and Clifford, R. M. (1990) *Infant/Toddler Environment Rating Scale*. New York: Teachers College Press.

Harms, T., Clifford, R. and Cryer, D. (1998) *Early Childhood Rating Scale: Revised Edition*. New York: Teachers College Press.

Hedges, H. (2003) Avoiding 'magical' thinking in children: the case for teachers' science subject knowledge, *Early Childhood Folio*, 7: 2–7.

Hendricks, A. and Meade, A. (with Wylie, C.) (1993) *Competent Children: Influences of Early Chilhood Experiences*. Pilot Study Report. Wellington: New Zealand Council for Educational Research and Faculty of Education, Victoria University of Wellington.

Hill, D., Reid, R. and Stover, S. (1998) More than educating children: the evolutionary nature of playcentre's philosophy of education, in S. Stover (ed.) *Good Clean Fun: New Zealand's Playcentre Movement*. Auckland: New Zealand Playcentre Federation.

HMSO (1967) *Children and their Primary Schools: A Report of the Central Advisory Council for Education (England)* (Plowden Report). London: HMSO.

Howes, C. (1986) Quality indicators for infant-toddler daycare. Paper presented at the annual meeting of the American Educational Research Association,

San Francisco, California. http://www.eric.ed.gov/PDFS/ED273385.pdf [Accessed 30 July 2011].

Hughes, B. (1989) *Flags and Building Blocks, Formality and Fun: One Hundred Years of Free Kindergarten in New Zealand*. Wellington: New Zealand Council for Educational Research.

Isaacs, S. (1933) *Social Development in Young Children*. London: Routledge and Kegan Paul.

Jordan, B. (2009) Scaffolding learning and co-constructing understandings, in A. Anning, J. Cullen and M. Fleer (eds) *Early Childhood Education: Society and Culture*, 2nd edition. London: Sage Publications.

Kanyal, M. and Cooper, L. (2012) Young children's perceptions of their classroom environment: perspectives from England and India, in T. Papatheodorou and J. Moyles (eds) *Cross-Cultural Perspectives on Early Childhood*. London: Sage Publications.

Katz, L. G. (1988) What should young children be doing?, *American Educator*, Summer: 29–44.

Laevers, F. (1994) *The Leuven Involvement Scale for Young Children LIS-YC Manual* (Experiential Education Series No. 1). Leuven: Centre for Experiential Education.

Lightfoot, C., Cole, M. and Cole, S. (2009) *The Development of Children*, 6th edition. New York: Worth Publishers.

Lincoln, Y. S. and Guba, E.G. (1985) *Naturalistic Inquiry*. Newbury Park, CA: Sage Publications.

LTS (Learning and Teaching Scotland) (2010) *Pre-Birth to Three*. http://www.ltscotland.org.uk/Images/PreBirthToThreeBooklet-tcm4-633448.pdf [Accessed 30 July 2011].

Luff, P. (2010) Ways of seeing and knowing children. Unpublished PhD thesis. Chelmsford: Anglia Ruskin University.

Luff, P. (2012) Challenging assessment, in T. Papatheodorou and J. Moyles (eds) *Cross-Cultural Perspectives on Early Childhood*. London: Sage Publications.

McDonald, G. (1974) Educational innovation: the case of the New Zealand playcentre, *New Zealand Journal of Educational Studies*, 9(2): 153–65.

McDonald, G. (1986) The use of video recording for the study of young children, *Early Childhood Folio*, 2, Item 13.

McMillan, B. and Meade, A. (1985) Observation: the basic techniques, *Research Information for Teachers*, Set 1, Item 7.

McMillan, M. (1919) *The Nursery School*. London: Dent.

McMurray, A. J., Pace, R. W. and Scott, D. (2004) *Research: A Commonsense Approach*. Southbank, Victoria: Thomson.

Mairs, K. (1990) *A Schema Booklet for Parents*. Corby: Pen Green Centre.

May, H. (1997) *The Discovery of Early Childhood: The Development of Services for the Care and Education of Very Young Children Mid-eighteenth Century Europe to Mid-twentieth Century New Zealand*. Auckland: Auckland University Press/Bridget Williams Books with New Zealand Council for Educational Research.

May, H. (2009) *Politics in the Playground: The World of Early Education in Postwar New Zealand*, revised editon. Dunedin: Otago University Press.

May, H. and Podmore, V. (2000) 'Teaching Stories': an approach to self-evaluation of early childhood programmes, *European Early Childhood Research Journal*, 8(1): 61–74.

Meade, A. and Staden, F. (1985) Once upon a time, amongst blocks and car cases: action research to enable girls' mathematical learning, *Research Information for Teachers*, Set 2, Item 5.

Miller, L., Rustin, M., Rustin, M. and Shuttleworth, J. (1989) *Closely Observed Infants*. London: Duckworth.

Ministry of Education (1996) *Te Whāriki: He Whāriki Mātauranga mō-ngā-Makapuna o Aotearoa: Early Childhood Curriculum*. Wellington: Learning Media. http://www.educate.ece.govt.nz/EducateHome/learning/curriculumAndLearning/TeWhariki.aspx [Accessed 30 July 2011].

Ministry of Education (2002) *Pathways to the Future/Ngä Huarahi Arataki*. Wellington: Learning Media.

Ministry of Education (2009) *Kei Tua o te Pae /Assessment for Learning: Early Childhood Exemplars*. Wellington: Learning Media. http://www.educate.ece.govt.nz/EducateHome/learning/curriculumAndLearning/Assessmentforlearning/KeiTuaotePae.aspx [Accessed 30 July 2011].

Moss, P. (2005) It's your choice, *Nursery World*, 24 November 2005 [Online] http://www.nurseryworld.co.uk/news/712059/Its-choice/ [Accessed 24 November 2009].

Mukherji, P. and Albon, D. (2010) *Research Methods in Early Childhood*. London: Sage Publications.

Mutch, C. (2005) *Doing Educational Research: A Practitioner's Guide to Getting Started*. Wellington: NZCER Press.

NAEYC (National Association for the Education of Young Children) (2005) *Code of Ethical Conduct and Statement of Commitment, Position Statement*. http://www.naeyc.org/files/naeyc/file/positions/PSETH05.pdf [Accessed 30 July 2011].

New Zealand Association for Research in Education (2010). *New Zealand Association for Research in Education Ethical Guidelines* (revised December 2010). http://www.nzare.org.nz/research-ethics.html [Accessed 24 August 2011].

Nutbrown, C. (2006) *Threads of Thinking: Young Children's Learning and the Role of Early Education*, 3rd edition. London: Sage Publications.

Nutbrown, C. and Carter, C. (2010) The tools of assessment: watching and learning, in G. Pugh and B. Duffy (eds) *Contemporary Issues in the Early Years*, 5th edition. London: Sage Publications.

Palaiologou, I. (2010) *The Early Years Foundation Stage: Theory and Practice*. London: Sage Publications.

Papatheodorou, T. and Luff, P. with Gill, J. (2011) *Child Observation for Learning and Research*. Harlow: Pearson.

Pascal, C. (2003) Effective early learning: an act of practical theory, *European Early Childhood Research Journal*, 11(2): 7–28.

Pascal, C. and Bertram, T. (1997) *Effective Early Learning: Case Studies in Improvement*. London: Hodder and Stoughton.

Pascal, C., Bertram, A. and Ramsden, F. (1994) *Effective Early Learning Research Project: The Quality Evaluation and Development Process*. Worcester: Worcester College of Higher Education.

Pascal, C., Bertram, A., Ramsden, F., Georgeson, J., Saunders, M. and Mould, C. (1996) *Effective Early Learning Research Project: Evaluating and Developing Quality in Early Childhood Settings. A Professional Development Programme*, 2nd edition. Centre for Early Childhood Research, Worcester College of Higher Education: Amber Publishing.

Penrose, P. (1998) *Take Another Look/Tirohia Ano: A Guide to Observing Children*, 2nd edition. Auckland: New Zealand Playcentre Federation.

Peters, S. (2009) Responsive reciprocal relationships: the heart of the *Te Whākiri* curriculum, in T. Papatheodorou and J. Moyles (eds) *Learning Together in the Early Years: Relational Pedagogy*. London: Routledge.

Piaget, J. (1968) *The Construction of Reality in the Child* (Translated by M. Cook). London: Routledge.

Piaget, J. and Inhelder, B. (1969) *The Psychology of the Child*. New York: Basic Books.

Podmore, V. N. (1978) Polynesian and Pākehā new entrant school children's classroom behaviour: an observational study. Unpublished MA thesis, Victoria University of Wellington, Wellington.

Podmore, V. N. (1984) Aspects of Māori and Pākehā mothers' interactions with their preschool children. Unpublished PhD thesis, Massey University, Palmerston North.

Podmore, V. N. (2009) Questioning evaluation quality in early childhood, in A. Anning, J. Cullen and M. Fleer (eds) *Early Childhood Education: Society and Culture*, 2nd edition. London: Sage Publications.

Podmore, V. N. and Craig, B. (1991) *Infants and Toddlers in New Zealand Childcare Centres*, Final Report. Wellington: New Zealand Council for Educational Research.

Podmore, V. and Craig, B. (1993) *Infants and Toddlers in the Childcare Centres of Aotearoa*. Wellington: New Zealand Council for Educational Research.

Podmore, V. N. and May, H. (with Mara, D.) (1998) *Evaluating Early Childhood Programmes Using the Strands and Goals of Te Whāriki, the National Early Childhood Curriculum*, Final Report on Phases One and Two to the Ministry of Education. Wellington: New Zealand Council for Educational Research and Ministry of Education.

Podmore, V. N. and Meade, A. (with Kerslake Hendricks, A.) (2000) *Aspects of Quality in Early Childhood Education*. Wellington: New Zealand Council for Educational Research.

Podmore, V., May, H. and Carr, M. (2001) The 'Child's Questions': programme evaluation with Te Whāriki using 'Teaching Stories', *Early Childhood Folio*, 5: 6–9.

Podmore, V. N., Wendt-Samu, T., Taouma, J. and Tapusoa, E. (2005) Language, culture, and community: action research with infants and young children at a Pasifika early childhood centre of innovation. Keynote address at the OMEP Asia-Pacific conference, December, Victoria University of Wellington, Wellington.

Pre-School Learning Alliance (2011) *Interview with Alliance Founder Belle Tutaev*. http://www.pre-school.org.uk/bellevideo [Accessed 30 July 2011].

Qualifications and Curriculum Authority (QCA) (2000) *Curriculum Guidance for the Foundation Stage*. London: DfES Publications.

Renwick, M. (1997) *Starting School: A Guide for Parents and Caregivers*. Wellington: New Zealand Council for Educational Research.

Richardson, L. (1998) Writing: a method of enquiry, in N. K. Denzin and Y. S. Lincoln (eds) *Collecting and Interpreting Qualitative Materials*. Thousand Oaks, CA: Sage Publications.

Rinaldi, C. (2006) *In Dialogue with Reggio Emilia: Listening, Researching and Learning*. London: RoutledgeFalmer.

Rogoff, B. (1990) *Apprenticeship in Thinking: Cognitive Development in Social Context*. New York: Oxford University Press.

Rogoff, B. (1998) Cognition as a collaborative process, in D. Kuhn and R. S. Siegler (eds) *Handbook of Child Psychology, Vol 2: Cognition, Perception, and Language*, 5th edition. New York: Wiley.

Rogoff, B. (2003) *The Cultural Nature of Human Development*. New York: Oxford University Press.

Rogoff, B., Mistry, J. J., Göncü, A. and Mosier, C. (1993) Guided participation in cultural activity by toddlers and caregivers, *Monographs of the Society for Research in Child Development*, 58 (8, Serial No. 236).

Rogoff, B., Baker-Sennett, J., Lacasa, P. and Goldsmith, D. (1995) Development through participation in sociocultural activity, in J. J. Goodnow, P. J. Miller and F. Kessel (eds) *Cultural Practices as Contexts for Development*. San Francisco, CA: Jossey-Bass.

Royal Tangaere, A. (1996) Māori human development learning theory, in B. Webber (ed) *He Paepae Kōrero: Research Perspectives in Māori Education*. Wellington: New Zealand Council for Educational Research.

Royal Tangaere, A. (1997) *Learning Māori Together: Kōhanga Reo and Home*. Wellington: New Zealand Council for Educational Research.

School Curriculum Assessment Authority (SCAA) (1996) *Nursery Education: Desirable Outcomes for Children's Learning on Entering Compulsory Education*. London: SCAA and DfEE Publications.

Scottish Executive (2005) *Curriculum for Excellence*. Edinburgh: Scottish Executive.

Scottish Executive/Learning and Teaching Scotland (2005) *Birth to Three. Supporting Our Youngest Children*. Edinburgh: Scottish Executive/LTS.

Sheridan, M.D. (1973) *Children's Development from Birth to Five Years: The Stycar Sequences*. Windsor: NFER.

Sheridan, M. D., Sharma, A. and Cockerill, H. (2008) *From Birth to Five Years: Children's Developmental Progress*, 3rd edition. London: Routledge.

Siraj-Blatchford, I. (2010) A focus on pedagogy: case studies of effective practice, in K. Sylva, E. Melhuish, P. Sammons, I. Siraj-Blatchford and B. Taggart (eds) *Early Childhood Matters*. Abingdon: Routledge.

Siraj-Blatchford, I., Sylva, K., Muttock, S., Gilden, R. and Bell, D. (2002) *Researching Effective Pedagogy in the Early Years*, Research Report RR356. London: Department for Education and Skills.

Siraj-Blatchford, I., Sylva, K., Laugharne, J., Milton, E. and Charles, F. (2006) *Monitoring and Evaluation of the Effective Implementation of the Foundation Phase (MEEIFP) Project Across Wales*, Evaluation Report. Cardiff: Welsh Assembly Government.

Smith, A. B. (1996) *The Quality of Childcare Centres for Infants in New Zealand*, State-of-the-Art Monograph No. 4. Palmerston North: Massey University, New Zealand Association for Research in Education.

Smith, A. B. (1998) *Understanding Children's Development*, 4th edition. Wellington: Bridget Williams Books.

Stephenson, A. (1999) *Opening Up the Outdoors: A Case Study of Young Children's Outdoor Experiences in One Childcare Centre*, Occasional Paper No. 4. Wellington: Institute for Early Childhood Studies, Victoria University of Wellington.

Sylva, K., Roy, C. and Painter, M. (1986) *Childwatching at Playgroup and Nursery School*. Oxford: Basil Blackwell.

Sylva, K., Melhuish, E., Sammons, P., Siraj-Blatchford, I. and Taggart, B. (2004) *The Effective Provision of Pre-School Education (EPPE) Project*, Final Report. London: DfES. https://www.education.gov.uk/publications/eOrderingDownload/SSU-FR-2004-01.pdf [Accessed 30 July 2011].

Te One, S. (2003) The context for te Whāriki: contemporary issues of influence, in J. Nuttall (ed.) *Weaving Te Whāriki: Aotearoa New Zealand's Early Childhood Curriculum Document in Theory and Practice*. Wellington: New Zealand Council for Educational Research.

Te One, S. (2005) Children's rights and early childhood policy: impacts and influences, *New Zealand Annual Review of Education*, 14: 171–94.

Thelen, E. and Adolph, K. E. (1992) Arnold L. Gesell: the paradox of nature and nurture, *Developmental Psychology*, 28 (3): 368–80.

Trowell, J. and Miles, G. (1991) The contribution of observation training to professional development in social work, *Journal of Social Work Practice*, 5(1): 51–60.

Tyler, S. (1979) *Keele Preschool Assessment Guide*, Keele University Library Occasional Publication No. 15. Keele: University of Keele.

Vasta, R., Haith, M. and Miller, S. (1999) *Child Psychology: The Modern Science*, 3rd edition. New York: John Wiley and Sons.

Vygotsky, L. S. (1978) *Mind in Society: The Development of Higher Mental Processes*. Cambridge, MA: Harvard University Press.

WAG (Welsh Assembly Government) (2008) *The Foundation Phase, 3–7*. Cardiff: Welsh Assembly Government.

Warming, H. (2005) Participant observation: a way to learn about children's perspectives, in A. Clark, A. T. Kjørholt and P. Moss (eds) *Beyond Listening*. Bristol: The Policy Press.

Warren, S. (1985) Researcher observes children, *Playcentre Journal*, 63: 6.

Webster, R. (2010) Listening to and learning from children's perspectives, in J. Moyles (ed.) *Thinking About Play: Developing a Reflective Approach*. Maidenhead: McGraw-Hill Education/Open University Press.

Weikart, D. P., Rogers, L., Adcock, C. and McClelland, D. (1971) *The Cognitively Oriented Curriculum: A Framework for Preschool Teachers*. Urbana, IL: University of Illinois.

Whalley, M. and the Pen Green Centre Team (2007) *Involving Parents in their Children's Learning*. London: Sage Publications.

Wood, D., Bruner, J. S. and Ross, G. (1976) The role of tutoring in problem solving, *Journal of Child Psychology and Psychiatry*, 17: 89–100.

Worthington, M. (2010) Play is a complex landscape: imagination and symbolic meanings, in P. Broadhead, J. Howard and E. Wood (eds) *Play and Learning in the Early Years*. London: Sage Publications.

Wylie, C., Thompson, J. and Kerslake Hendricks, A. (1996) *Competent Children at 5: Families and Early Education*. Wellington: New Zealand Council for Educational Research.

Wylie, C., Thompson, J. and Lythe, C. (2001) *Competent Children at 10: Families, Early Education, and Schools*. Wellington: New Zealand Council for Educational Research.

Zeni, J. (2001) *Ethical Issues in Practitioner Research*. New York: Teachers College, Columbia University.

Index

Locators shown in *italics* refer to tables.